POLY

NEW SPECULATIVE WRITING

POLY

NEW SPECULATIVE WRITING

LEE BALLENTINE EDITOR

OCEAN VIEW BOOKS

MOUNTAIN VIEW CALIFORNIA

Library of Congress Cataloging-in-Publication Data

Poly : new speculative writing / Lee Ballentine, editor ;
   [contributors, Diane Ackerman et al.]
      p.   cm.
     Bibliography: p.
     ISBN 0-938075-08-X — ISBN 0-938075-05-5 (pbk.)
     1. Science fiction poetry, American. 2. Science fiction poetry,
English. I. Ballentine, Lee. II. Ackerman, Diane.
PS595.S35P64 1989
808.81'356—dc19   87-19827
                                                                CIP
                                                                (rev.)

© 1989 Ocean View Books
Box 4148, Mountain View CA 94040

Printed in the United States of America

First Edition

1 2 3 4 5 6 7 8 9 10   95 94 93 92 91 90 89

The era of literary movements has passed, undoubtedly. Manifestos, cultural and otherwise, are passé. Wyndham Lewis's *Blast* for example, now much too valuable to own, is quite impossible to read today as we might have late in June, 1914. Still we can imagine that Lewis would find little to bless and much to *blast* in a time when text is almost entirely transient. Comic books, disintegrating magazines, and screen-scrolled texts are the rule. Or no text at all. Books themselves are not taken seriously by large segments of our society.

Yet in an age of 100-channel television, the compact disc, the on-line database, you're holding a cultural artifact of a type even you may believe defunct, having in all likelihood paid a high price for it. All of which should come as no surprise in an age formed by the expectations of a full generation of science fiction readers.

Recall that until recent anthropologic time, human ideas were propagated one-at-a-time, in conversation, banter, or sheer hollering. Since hearing and remembering are such doubtful mechanisms, it was inevitable that new techniques would be improvised, and chief among them, text. One thing seems certain—long after text was pervasive, books continued to be owned only by initiates in the esoterica of writing, and by others with the wealth to command them. Cost, not physical repression, has always been the best means of keeping information under control— the high cost of producing texts *and the immensely higher cost of teaching people to read them.* Unreading populations still dominate the planet. Ground has been lost, even in reading zones, where text has been all-but-supplanted by video among previously literate subgroups. Since our 1960s evening news videotapes have long since been bulk-erased, we find ourselves in a retrograde phase, creating history out of old technologies—text, and even memory, an old technology indeed.

Text may have spent much of its cultural and political energy, but it retains hermetic force. It conjures the early, indigestible ideas which are destined either to sink without a trace, or to be transformed into mass-media pablum. So, though they have arrived very late, relatively affordable computer software, laser printers, and cassette duplicators have some potential for indirect impact, giving *samizdat* the opportunity to look respectable enough for middle-of-the-road book buyers. Once abroad in the world, the stuff has a chance at least of falling into interested hands.

It may be worthwhile to recall that these developments are only the latest in a series of dramatic reductions in the cost of text. As school-children used to learn, German technology leaped forward in the 15th century. Books for the first time could be created and owned not only by the great monastic houses, but by lesser, even dissident institutions. Within 30 decades, such inventions as magazines, the novel, and advertising slogans were commonplace. London's *Tatler* appeared in 1709, the *Spectator* in 1711, and the *Gentleman's Magazine* in 1731. Milton, in the 1640s, was among the first to refer to "the novel" in a way approaching its modern sense. It was left to the 20th century, however, to cover every surface, from wineglasses to jet aircraft, with ads.

Today, texts are once again difficult to find, this time because of their abundance. Billions of books exist, and millions of them contain useful ideas or information we can know only as rumor. Life is not long enough to find them, much less read them. Against this deluge, we have raised such institutions as book clubs, the public library, and of course, popular criticism, which can be defined as the profession of disposing of texts through unattention.

Among some constituencies which were left unrepresented in academe—the book selling cartel, publishing and other agenda'd institutions—the alienation of being buried under a mountain of ideas with no way to find the useful ones led to the development of new choice algorithms. Unclassical thinkers began to burrow in the all-surrounding text in order to make something of it. Radical steps were taken in the direction of the *found*. The surrealists and their predecessors were early in the game. Dada ripped newspapers into strips and Tristan Tzara pulled poems out of hats. Surrealists jumbled type-faces, played Exquisite Corpse, started small presses and re-discovered trance automatism, while lone innovators like Artaud turned madness, drugs, or drunkenness into similar filters. All took, in common with the critics they despised, the task of converting the 20th century's leviathan of text into a human-sized experience.

Almost in parallel, early explorers of genre fiction were working through their own alienation. In the Gernsback era (though contemporary scholarship has borne-out the common-sense conclusion that science fiction predates *RALPH 124C 41*), enthusiast presses began to publish the writing that would evolve into modern science fiction. Despite the parallels, American science fiction has, for most of its history, remained wholly apart from the mainstream of literary praxis.

In the margins and under the fly-leaves of science fiction, however, a new kind of speculative writing has recently begun to appear. Although it spans drama and fiction, its literary focus is most evident in its poetry. Because poetry "doesn't sell," those who work in it have relative freedom to innovate, at least as fully within science fiction as outside. But this speculative poetry is not exactly science fiction poetry, a form which appeared in the 1940s, peopled with space cadets and endangered by killer-asteroids. When the new wave of science fiction came along in the 1950s, the associated poetry held tight to traditional verse forms. Later, a few writers, including some represented in *POLY*, began exploring the future in the context of modern poetry. As the term *speculative fiction* was coined by those wishing to keep cliches at arm's length, so with poetry.

A debt to the model *speculative philosophy* can be read in the phrase as well. Kant and Kierkegaard. Speculative poetry is not content to explore the minutiae treated by sex-lives-of-the-wealthy-poetry, or linguistic-angel-counting-poetry. Rather, it is willing to engage death, politics, the nature of meaning, themes taken from the wide-cast net of science fiction.

At the same time, it is poetry for its own sake. Having in many cases confronted the crisis of modernism on science's home ground, speculative poetry is not "about" its themes. The surrealists seem to have been the first in the outside world to take notice of science fiction, early praising H.P. Lovecraft et al. But although there are mutual influences, speculative poetry is not equivalent to surrealism, the invisible totem in contemporary life which, against all odds, continues to thrive though in corrupted form. Would television, for example, be effective without the pervasive surrealism that underpins it? Its brilliant non sequitur commercials, its impossible dramas, the music-video? Surrealism is a fact, it just happens to be a fact too obvious to notice. We in the eighties are living surrealism.

Meanwhile, biology and astronomy were becoming fertile grounds for poets. Science poetry, modern poetry that makes use of the themes or language of science without necessarily having a futurist focus, is close-kin to the speculative. Birkhauser and Science-85 published a fine collection, *Songs From Unsung Worlds*. In its early pages, Alan Lightman and George Starbuck discuss the divergence of science and poetry. They err primarily in their premise, for poetry *is a science*, an exact science, akin to astronomy. The *accidentals* of poetry are exactly parameterized;

are functions mapped onto emotion, knowledge, or a series of events. They are no *accident*. A Chinese poet, say, Li Shang-yin, was master of his literary allusions. Each important ideogram defined by the context of its every previous occurrence in the classical canon. Like a pre-atomic physicist consulting his iridium meter block, Li might choose with effect a character used only six times before in his literature. With a fraction the memes of classical Chinese, our contemporary languages are perforce, more statistical, more quantum mechanical.

Just as Kepler assimilated Brahe's observations, H.P. Lovecraft mined the bizarre reports of Charles Fort. To create art from the contemporary blizzard of texts, words, radio-voices, poets today must be sifters of data, expert auditors. Since sifting only in the academic preserve, like hunting game in a zoo, skews the results, they must listen on the street, eavesdrop. So evolved Beat and Funk and Punk poetries. With few meaningful standards of literary education, our society has left its poets the only scientists of human expression who practice in the field.

Poets *are scientists*, and scientists must be anarchists. Their only rule, argues philosopher Paul Feyerabend—*anything goes*. That at their best, scientists are also poets, seems too clear a fact to be doubted by any but themselves. If *you* doubt it, open any good Topology text at random, and read a theorem or two.

Of course, the science of poetry differs from its cognate disciplines. Poets, more than chemists, more than teachers or factory workers, must go their own way, with no training programs, no reliable route through the profession, no tenure. Poets nearly always work alone, often live alone. They are paid little for their work. To survive, they band together, publish together; but because their higher need is solitude, their collectives crumble, they repudiate their manifestos. Like chemistry, poetry is a dangerous profession. Sometimes poets love or hate each other, marry or murder one another. Sometimes they do not survive.

Like the rest of us, the artists represented in *POLY* are struggling with a myriad of troubles. Some are domestic, personal—but these do not occupy much of their attention. It is problems that are large and futurist, that haven't yet begun to trouble us, that have long been with us, or that look like they will be with us for a long time *if* we survive that are the raw material of this writing.

Like all literature of the future, speculative writing is, on some level, really of the present. We write what we know, and cannot do otherwise, and what we know is our own time. It seems the nature of our time that, when poetic elements fuse most effectively, the view of the future obtained is frequently dark, deadly, frightening.

The new speculative writing *isn't* the sole province of those represented here, and many here do not seek, or even accept, the designation. To develop a sense of what it *is*, we need to take a long look at its cognates, at what it is-not-quite. *POLY* is an attempt to do that, as a loose-drawn net collecting many voices. In the entente between science and surrealism, the cross-pollination that *POLY* is, the incision of surrealism, the introspection of modern poetry, the vocabulary of the sciences, and a measure of science fiction's enthusiasm, are all engaged with the theme of *the future*.

Lee Ballentine

CONTENTS

lives and writes in Denver. A veteran of the science fiction magazines, he is best known for his short fiction, and cites the following stories among his favorites: "The Unfortunate Mr. Morky" (*The 8th Annual of the Year's Best SF*, edited by Judith Merril, Simon and Schuster 1963), "An Adventure in the Yolla Bolly Middle Eel Wilderness" (*The Best from Fantasy and Science Fiction 19th Series*, edited by Edward L. Ferman, Doubleday 1971), and "Sylvester's Revenge" (*The Science Fiction Weight-Loss Book*, edited by Isaac Asimov, Crown 1983). Aandahl's novellas, *Midnight Snack* and *Deathmatch in Disneyland*, have recently appeared in *Fantasy & Science Fiction*.

Vance
Aandahl

BEETLE-HAIRED idiot boy
nine days hunted in the brittle-needled heat
your tightening stomach heavy with hunger
your dim mind blazing with too much light
turn your creep to the dark arroyo
move in your pain like the humming sun
edge numbly through manzanita   mesquite
where chaparral turns to brush & brush to jungle
crawl hands & knees
down the sluggish creek
dank   overgrown with reeds
slimy with frogs and slugs
the few wrinkles of your walnut brain still sizzling
a hot mosquito buzz in this deepest of shades
rise trembling to your feet
see the dripping creekbank cave where the owleaters sleep

YOUR VACANT head shimmers with blurs of white light
but you know they're there
their eyes glowing like snake eggs
softer than milk in a cool black hole
& this time beetle-haired idiot boy
you won't run

IN THAT same shimmer of cottonmouth eyes
my wife's brother's wife
lifts backwards with her head
a comic fall   promising much laughter
    at impact the glasses bolt from her face
    a jolt just hard enough to rupture bloodlines
she has time   time to stand
time to walk back to the patio
even time to speak once   reaching out
around the pain of her crushed scalp   to chide us
once   before blood darkens her brain

YOU KNOW she is hurt
in the light of these dead white eyes
in the whispers of the hunters above the thorn ridge
in the roots   in the mulch
in the flattened grass   in the tremolo of pain
running frenzied through your disappearing stomach
& when the owleaters sidle from their cave
& clamber up the creekbank   jabbering
swinging their arms like gibbons   you cannot help
but follow   cannot help but flee the pain

THEIR PANTING slows as the sun goes down
      dusk   silence   & the owls come
at first only the susurrus of wings
a movement of shadow in the twisted juniper
a horned blur curving through the corner of your eye
      then the owleaters break back their heads
stretching their necks to the darkening sky
& two by two the owls swoop down
locking their talons on the strained-up collarbones
flaming their wings in a pinesap fury
stabbing open the upturned throats with their beaks
mating into the wounds   feather & blood blurring
a dark vibrating hemorrhage of pain

THE PIÑONS blink silver   the owls are gone
the owleaters slowly sway down
their gaping throats grown shut with plumage
      feathers frothing back
over their shoulders   down their arms
      great wings
soft & shuddering in the darkening night
they lift & drop   lift & drop
grounded by their own clumsiness
till they find the steadier certain flap
& lurch away   colliding with treetops
      in the lower air

Vance
Aandahl

4

Vance
Aandahl

THE SAME reptilian air
     here in the false light of the intensive care ward
     where Joyce sinks in a rig of tubes
     her eyelids puffy & not quite closed
the same lower reptilian air that cools her lungs
cools mine too   & yours
for you are me and we are here together
but hunted beetle-haired idiot boy
your owleaters will not come to the hospital brain
no they're not here   they're not here

poet and futurist, divides her year between Ithaca 14850 and St. Louis 63130. She has won many awards for her poetry, including a Pushcart Prize, the Black Warrior Review Poetry Prize, and Cornell's Academy of American Poets Poetry Prize. Her poems have been read in *Ambit*, *Paris Review*, *Science 84*, *New Letters*, and Robert Frazier's anthology, *Burning With a Vision*, and heard in Jon Lomberg's 1975 radio series *Ideas into the Universe*, on CBC Toronto. Her *POLY* poems are new to print.

In 1979 and 1980, Ackerman served as poetry researcher for the *Cosmos* television series, and since 1980 she has been a member of the advisory board of The Planetary Society. Her book publications: *The Planets: A Cosmic Pastorale* (1976), *Wife of Light* (1978), *Twilight of the Tenderfoot* (1980), and *Lady Faustus* (1983), all from William Morrow. Recent books are *On Extended Wings* (Atheneum 1985) and *Reverse Thunder* (Lumen 1985).

1

Diane
Ackerman

Was that the dream, the birds clubbing up
in the trees? This vigil beside a lagoon of stars

as night pools with dank luminosity?
The timberline pines all pointing upward

and the eye flowing from ground to treetop,
then pausing. . .what a long leap into the sky.

But so easy, a voice like falling leaves
whispers, *just lean into nothing. Learn to let go.*

2

When I think of the dream, I think of days
like this one, when heat shimmer

over the trapped lucidity of the pool
is more august and certain than any creed.

Should I believe in the capital of Poland
or in those lozenges of light?

Which is irrefutable, WORK = ENERGY × DISTANCE
or in those lozenges of light?

Which testimony is older, which temper
would you harness, what rapture is steeper

than those lozenges of light, in which all
the lost logarithms of the sun vibrate?

3

Was that the dream, then, any late afternoon,
when Japanese beetles couple

Diane
Ackerman

on the grape leaves, and the crows sound
like they're choking in the trees?

Then a milt of stars vented across the night,
a dribble from some early rage of the Universe

whose sunglow tantrum became wheat, became blood.
John Clare used to go out looking for the horizon,

where sunlight walked a tightrope,
and the air was thin as a razor. I have found it

in the savory curve of this summer day, a dry heat
I love with almost palpable poignancy.

4

When I wonder what the dream was,
I think of the cell-by-cell furnace

of a man's skin, how he strikes the flint
in my hips to a self-quenching flame.

Was that the dream, the genteel treacheries
of the flesh, the daily acts of quiet terror

an engaged heart defines? We dip into our wells
and churn up slaggy water, then search

our reflection in each other's well:
the hallucination of a facebone,

the red benediction of blood below the surface,
the sweet penitentiary of the body,

whose bones we grip from within,
crying our innocence, begging for release.

Diane
Ackerman
His touch makes sound leap from my skin,
as he mulls the cool, flowing cider of my limbs.

The steam that rises has syntax,
sends words down my spine.

5

Was that the dream, then, a man
who welds your body to his with a look?

He walks across the room. Around his neck
hangs the amulet of your desire.

He has an average build and an average face,
but his hand is large enough

to hold a live, beating heart. Was that the dream,
the banana republic of love,

where petty tyrants sweep one away
by nightfall for some gentle terror?

6

When I puzzle over the dream
that could stay a devout watcher,

rifle loaded, in the duck shoot
of self-esteem, waiting

for one's own dazzling array to ambush,
I think of apple trees,

so deformed in the cold months,
wearing Halloween masks, limbs hunched and gnarled.

You marvel blossom could irrupt,
let alone ripe fruit. And I think of athletes

Diane
Ackerman

blowing across the grass like seeds,
anonymous, possessive, able to hold ground,

but yielding fully to each sway
in the hurtled, thin harmonies of motion.

7

The invisible line of a fisherman
gesturing toward the out-running surf—

Was that the dream? A roux of fish eggs
pearled among seaweed—Was that the dream?

The stampede of birds and mice
pumping their white forevers—Was that the dream?

What the hockey goalie knows
who, lion-maned as a Kabuki dancer,

falls on his knees, proposing to the goal—
Was that the dream?

The mind whirrs, the world inters—
Was that the dream? A code whistled

underwater—Was that the dream?
Our castle of desire

set in a kingdom of disappointment—
Was that the dream?

Diane
Ackerman

8

When I wonder what the dream was
that began with outcry, and will end

with the cold mummery of bare bones,
I fix on the brown bark of shag hickories,

the sultry drawl that's summer heat,
and all the innuendos of bird and light

that make a mental breeze in the weather
of one's life, where a mass murderer

is far more explicable than a tree.
But was that the dream—shimmery patterns

in the heart's pulsarium, like constellations
tumbling from no height to no depth?

Diane
Ackerman

In white gowns of winter,
nurses rush like chill
down corridors pale as waning
light, to circulate
among the semi-private rooms
with a quiver of needles
and a pyramidal smile:
the calm apaches who broadcast hope.

He watches from the unbearable
comfort of his bed
the lake angering like a shield
in the hazy fall sun.
And he remembers the deer
who leap into his yard
like lengths of cedar wood
to paw fermented apples
and browse the raspberry shoots.

A piece of him pulls free
and circles with fringed wings,
looking down through bald sky
to the Amazon of wires and tinctures
where he lies, to the white smocks
appearing like lilies each day,
to the field of white phlox
where, unbridled, his cells
gallop in all directions.

Diane
Ackerman

of the overlapping waves, boiling surf
    into a green-grey howl,
the waves rearing up like cobras to strike,
    then sighing back from the lips of the boardwalk,
as waves, thick as rolling whales,
    spume white and roll again and spume again,
the waves habitués watch from blanket or deck chair,
    with a patience powerful as thick green glass:
the cabaret of petticoats: the waves rolling
    without plot or purpose, as we will be in time,
without plot or purpose: which is why the gulls glide
    like a pair of brackets overhead,
and the waves run like herds of white mice
    between the hypnotic tantrums of the surf.

Andrei Codrescu writes in the *Baltimore Sun*, "Argüelles is genuine."
This premise is borne out in each of his six books, *Instamatic Recondi-
tioning* (Damascus Road 1978), *The Invention of Spain* (Downtown Poets
Co-op 1978), *Captive of the Vision of Paradise* (Hartmus Press 1981),
The Tattooed Heart of the Drunken Sailor (Ghost Pony Press 1982), his
Silverfish Review Poetry Chapbook Competition prize book, *Manicomio*
(1983), and *Nailed to the Coffin of Life* (Ruddy Duck Press 1984). He
has published in *American Poetry Review*, *Kayak*, *Atticus Review*,
Abraxas, and *Velocities*.

POLY   What facts of personal history, real or imagined, shed light
on the central problems of focus of your work?

Argüelles   Growing up amazed, like an outsider, in this 20th cen-
tury America...My father is a Mexican painter who saw Trotsky's
brains. Amen.

WONDERING WHAT HEAVEN SOUNDS LIKE AFTER DEATH

Ivan
Argüelles

an intelligent guess this side of reason
a shadow of a doubt a friend in need to the end
a cup of coffee is grist for the mill language
abdicates its use under the thumbnail twice removed
spectra of invisible colors ghosts of unborn children
hair and nerve tooth and file the indicators of time
stripped of their location an indivisible number
stamped in fire on the brow of the Creator
who nodding stumbling and fumbling falls
the pit opens the wheels turn the sky cracks
I can never remember into how many pieces
hunger thirst then sleep a prelude to dying
lawns of innocence an eye shuts on the cloud of its mind

what does it mean if I dont hear the music?
I am listening but to what?
the second movement begins when I least expect it
drills and saws and hammers and the cries of lost children
I choose just a sequence but forget beginning and end
a dense reflection captures me in its glass
there is scope here for more violins for sex
unintuited for literatures and basic harmony
there is room here for the invention of the wheel
for the age of the soul to dress itself in death
for the environmental tragedy of hell to be investigated
but that music which I no longer hear where is it?

in the ear of my eyelid I notice the tensions rising
piece-meal horizons of sound metallic dull flat temporal
do I sleep in the knee of the Creator dreaming huge grasses
blackening burnt wasted in the system of arteriosclerosis?
it is only sister greater older more unformed and uninformed
following me through the unfolding river of tragedy
she speaks she lifts her hands and wands and welcomes fate
an infinitesimal zone where the two of us observe the snow
gather on the table where the dung-cakes harden
strange that we no longer perceive how easily the sun
sets in that terrible violet hash of light beyond the hair-line

a gun goes off a thunder peal a detonation of nightmare
sounds we no longer hear absorbed by the music we cannot hear

a last look NO a last longing attempt to catch the echo

Ivan
Argüelles

Ivan
Argüelles

silhouettes of silver spikes jut into the ether
sky's multiple masks are shed like transparent skins
wet and darkening in the descent through shafts of smoke
to where you and I sit tied to the inconvenience of life
victims of a mad prince whose sanskrit titles roll on
into seas of goldenrod and teak
madness of this sort lasts for years between the frame
where the bone links to the beggar's hand
and the situation where the amir on his fifty cushions
prays that the prophet may deliver him from scrutiny
verses that have no beginning or end unfold
from the intricate mouthpiece of the psychoanalyst
who watched his lady die for three infinite hours
comfort never comes to those who still shake

a seed is needed a black pod a porous grain
from which the deity will emerge blue as a dolphin
to make amends between ourselves while the music lasts
we enter luminous rooms with tools deep in our heads
the walls change shape and color becomes convex
a film unreels slowly crazily between the immense shadows
of planets in conflict while gold-fish surface in the eye
of the hypnotist reclining in the image of the cathedral
doors reverse themselves in flight
a wind comes from an ancient field that used to be a city
or rather ten cities layered like gloves on the earth
antiquities dark and cuprous cast their baleful reflections
on the pool where we steep our worn feet

nothing comes back from the first rain
clouds massive as the child's memory of horses
gather for a conference above the buzzing mills
a water is extended across the entire eastern horizon *Ivan*
blind bonzes in glowing orange robes attend the mutilation by desire *Argüelles*
which is the remaining rite to be performed
something inside our brains turns to grainy light
small beings dense as melted gold dance against the surface
of what we see until the membranes become fluted withered
external rather than internal and the blood
shatters like glass somewhere deep within the echo

IN THE VALLEY OF THE PHARAOH OF THE SHADOW

Ivan
Argüelles

as in a ruin of sleep or water the sand rises
against the image of the moon's cold and distant flame

must press the wall must shake the edge of its line
adjacent the mind devours its reflection in self-love

when before did we step here on the traces of cities
asleep looking with our hands for the stones' engravings?

what angel dressed in the dread garments of absent seas
guides us to the Column where the law of the unending spheres burns?

as in a rust of language and thought and unrepeatable verse
the air lifts its manacles against the revolution of ice

LOST IN THE GEHENNA OF THE INFINITE CHILDHOOD THE EYE
speaks to the mildewed compass of the ears of time

the artillery of the mosque is aimed at the vacancies
we are bereft of passports and have no idea of Palestine

a strange god a minstrel decayed and profoundly lyrical
a beacon lit in the tomb of the soul of anthropomorphism

something is gnawing on the first letter of the alphabet
something is burying its bone in the terrific hurdle of OMEGA

the house of stale water must be moved from its pre-history
the arbor of skeleton trees must be heaved from pure sight

heaven's timbers are on fire the foundations are BOTTOM
a river a single vein a line fading on rose-paper a sigh

echo symbol ether tense come to us passing like a needle
through the hair's ancient ear its valley of syllables unreconciled

Ivan
Argüelles

Beware of nothing respect the debased love the offal
Be dejected for being elect and supreme and knowing

the lost children their heads on the bar their gazes spent
a new phone-number system cannot revive them nor memory of the gods

Ivan
Argüelles

a simple melody derived from the black sea of music
she repeats her threnody her step her grave attitude
the light falls like a towel from her brow her mind
is naked beating with frail and agitated leaves
the water strikes its course the rain's legend turns to glass
she repeats the shape of her feet in beds of dust
in her   eyes the opposite shore of the meadow of death
shines pastoral inviting terrible and sweet through
which   come and go the uninvited gypsies with violins
tuned to the key of Delta and she passes through the note
repeating with her naked mind the song of Jesus' son
heroin coursing through the vein of her left wrist
recreates the myth of SLEEP the grand and eloquent
who speaks in the tongue of the Great Turk bereft of ears
for sailing to jerusalem backwards in the time of fasting
ceaseless in her rhythm she repeats the cause of metals
the shining things embedded thoughtlessly in the abyss
the careers of silver and gold extinguished on her tongue
her hands grasp invisible ideas about the dark melody
horses stop to eat the tickets of her fingers as she passes
silently into the curtains of mist and shadow beyond
the point fixed in her eyes as her hair wrapped
in an envelope of sand burns without being consumed
on her lips the questions about the soul's other half
about the naming of the Temple and the Morning Star
about the coffins of smoke named Sokrates the Beloved
and other pressing questions flicker like liquid torches
her hips are possessed of the greater meter her waist
undulates in the fixed prism of the unbidden number
it is India it is Cathay it is the silk road of the Khan
her mind her naked mind tossing with the percussion of fish
blind with human mouths that swim between her breasts
SUCH A ONE AS THIS WE FOUND ON THE HIGHWAY
   IN THE AMERICA OF DREAMS
she speaks mexican in whispers to the railroad agents
she sleeps in the ditch with her bare drum her belly
she repeats in the course of an hour the day of the meridian
zenith and quicksilver the virtue clothes too fast to wear!

of San Francisco, has played chess for a living, sold books and record albums, and worked in a public library and as an engineer in Silicon Valley. His poems have been published frequently in *Velocities* (Berkeley), *NRG* (Portland), *Star*Line* (Nantucket), and in *Mississippi Mud* and *Abraxas*. Other poems have been chosen for the *Portland Review* science fiction poetry issue (1981), and the Owlflight Press anthology *Aliens & Lovers*. Ballentine is the author of two books of poems, *Directional Information* (Ocean View Books) and *Basements in the Music-Box* (Xexoxial Editions), and is the editor of *POLY*.

Lee
Ballentine

Now opens the muscle of the heart
with a noise that plaits her brain into a weapon
and scabs that are weapons
taking voice in the bruised colors
polishing a bone of the body
until it reflects light
&—slips from between other ribs.

Astronomers—
more than your screensfull of pictures
O—Mars is more than your arid robot-ladle
scooping up ashes—there are yet
two arches of Automatism we must span.
One—dried in an infinite mudcracked sea
tangled in regions of cloud—

is useless for real travel.
The other is octagon—pineal
the route of the razor.
A child shall sing the penalties of his foe
only while SVENGALI listens.
Between the lids of his eyes
pure air flows into diamonds—diamonds!

All the panes of glass are thrumming.
The nerves that stretch in them are pain-songs
and long polarity
and overhead the white sun bows them
knots within them bellow
each instant the grained light unknots them
something comes visible—a yellow grimace
my flame caught cru-white—wavering
sick-slow entropy.

On the photovolt clock not a number flickers.
Seed carriers drift and slow to the pedestal
above the famous glass booth—
floating in a column of grain
the folds of my garment gathered at throat and hips
you have seen me—my closed eyes
smoke spelling out in dead script
and faint parallel text—
Sycorax-son.

A dry air stirs the pavilion—
a moth flutters at the bench
its wing bloom urged open
specimen pin frozen at its thorax
outside monitors lens on the puncture
each year one frame-scan is preserved
a gamma counter is trained-on through the glass
Argier poises its disputed calendar
on the rise in heart rate of my trapped fly.

Lee
Ballentine

Lee
Ballentine

Once—beside the glass booth
priests censing its corners
a crack in one wall widened by touch
the vault is festooned with old antlers
the color of crushed walnuts
a tank crew fires gatling rounds
at a tattered poster touting opium—
an old man in a coat charged with crescents
turns his audience inward to the glass.

(Singing and strange masks.)
So ends our dramatus of the Tempest
still the ship HELD-BREATH
is waiting her recruits!
—*Tell us of all the worlds you've seen!*
(The boy inside seems motionless—to speak.)
O—I have seen that rotting place Otranto
in pocks of her old landing field
murder and duel are practised—

—*Tell us of Argier!*
(Why do you pause and choke? Why do you
change grey as if to crumple into ash?)
Otranto! —the spacefield
mess of open containers and downpour of sweet fluid.
I became a ventriloquist
lips muscled—shouting
spume yawing in its descent—head snapping . . . .
—*Tell us of Argier!*

O—I have seen that city of Argier—
There are no windows where the bombs are made
but eyeless walls—the runnels of the armada
and a long journey to find me
in a tattered pavilion no longer guarded
at the center of that place—
the booth stands quite dark
bursts of occasional grey light
and no audience.

A newer instrument trained-on outside—
my moth still flutters its wings in the jar
and the grained light is steady
not a number has passed the clock
the designator half-shadowed—
how many places Setebos are in the recurrence?
in a column of air a boy flies wholly still—
dreaming a dream of his mother
gravid with Caliban—

Near a strange island
her ship has collapsed—
in shouting and bursts of gunfire
swimmers are swept off ...
—*How many stars fly through*
the starry hydrogen night?
a billion—billion—billion?
Still are the proofs of ventriloquism lacking—
look! —how the child's eyes are open!

Lee
Ballentine

*Lee
Ballentine*

In times now passed there ruled over the far-flung races of people an iron
fate with silent force. A dark and heavy blindfold. The ocean's dark green
depths were a goddess' lap. In crystal grottos an exuberant people revelled.
It was Death who interrupted this revelry with fear and dread and tears.

Novalis—Hymns to the Night

I. T E A R S

Grimes of exposure layered and lost in dry skin.
Rays of old distraction in his face
and pellucid tears
like the shark's blood savored in ALERON.
The drained husks tossed back thrashing.
Season gives place to autumn—and those left behind
trace diseases rising in the skin.
Rose and pallor couple.

Opposite oceans strain together
piling-up empires of liquid weight.
Through smashed canals the century tides
rush unimpeded. To live one must leave
and pass bored years on KETEX
or watch the stranded by transmission.

I I.

Today—two boys found a fabulous robe
in an urn of chalcedony.
A camera trained on the ruins of the old commune.
A robe of feathers
and an archive from a column recently fallen
A prison log of the commune.
Today—communards sent the robe
to fly in correct orbit
in a niche in the missile KETEX.

ALARIC shoved his friend
rubbed one hand in a fold of his suit
and grinned to touch the six small feathers there.
Later—when he pricked his thumb
at the point of one of them
he was afraid of the bright thoughts
coursing through his body.
He was afraid to become KAIL.

Lee
Ballentine

I I I.   S T A L L E N F A S T

The air having stilled—the muzzein
began low in each man's chest by induction.
GESTA rolled-up one leg of her court pyjamas
displaying the bud of her impatience
and though he was not young
KAIL felt the strength of a boy.

He sold his seat at the trading tables
under the shadow of the blue mosque
at STALLENFAST where weapons are coin.
Engines to floresce thoughts
and render treason visible.
To sever thumbs or solve an equation.

And in drab years they bought and raised two sons.
In the black years of destruction
they sheltered in the Necropolis
thinking sometimes of the body-son
they had given into service in the mosque.
Passed through the circle of vendors.
Passed-in as an infant
at a window stopped with a dossel of smoky glass
smaller than the book GESTA was made
to write his name in.

Lee
Ballentine

ALARIC woke with a sickness of luminous desert.
Of clear dwellings etched by sand.
A memory of bright rays oscillating
and structures melted through the city.
The nightly flight of agents
falling symphonies of dislocation.
Most of all GESTA's short hair and full breasts.

He woke more careful than his thirteen years.
Wise in gambler's virtue
and as protective of the remaining feathers.
In the end it was decided to pair him
with his sister ANOBEL—to cure him of his desire.
She honed it to a weapon.

IV.   PRAYERS AND TRANSMISSIONS

A single arc of radio scanning bluffs and sea
vibing an oil-drum in its nest of shell
and dirty pilings battered—battered.
Careful pips rising on the screen
slim and accipitral.

O ANOBEL my sister
sweep from the night's round belly
oblations of anxious noise
to be gentled in the radio dish
slipping through higher amplitudes
to spend their sullen energies at nodes of love.

Travelling up his sky-tether
ALARIC smells the first high throbs of rain.

A globe fell suddenly under the great rock   *Lee*
                                                                   Ballentine
shaped like a tiger. That evening
the pilot spared a young officer sent against her
and turned her last charge on the granite.
At length she made a home with her gaolers.

Her son STALLEN found his mother's cut
laid his hand within the stone
&—dreamed in furious beauty
of a satellite past heaven.
Of how as an old man he hid the shame
of his hundred daughters
and no sons—in the desert of eagles.

STALLEN woke and dug a well
and a town beside the well
and called them AGOULYESH.

His enemies called it STALLENFAST.
He began to carve the notched rock
into the shape of a tiger.

To hollow it and fill it with pleasures.
Inside he tiled it white covered with tracing.
Outside a pale blue.
The chemistry of his compulsion.
His chemists made a robe too narrow for his shoulders.

ALARIC awoke within the circum of the blue
palace—not yet a mosque.

Lee
Ballentine

Coiled in the people's satellite
in the chamber of self-criticism
ALARIC conjures heat.
He jabs the point of the sixth feather
pressing the sagging breasts of old GESTA
in his pilgrimage.

Aeons of brine wash over him
leaching virtues from his folds of rag.
Pity and seamanship
in capillary action.

Blood courses down.
Tea from a holed samovar
or pearls of sanguine memory.
A woman's severed thumbs
nailed on the great door
of the Necropolis.

A book naming his sons.
The petitions of the damned.
Too late life returns to the green planet.

Sparks leap the syntonized universe
groaning through layers of cloth.
Struck from the anvil of unmoved space
from this lonely station—to erase
the chill alignment of his mitochondria
to erase the woods and mosques—
and any urge vulnerable to him.

has read his poems in Australia, Denmark, Hungary, New Zealand, Sweden, and West Germany, and with Stephen Scobie as the Sound Poetry ensemble *Re:Sounding.* Among his eleven books of poems are *A Poem as Long as the Highway* (Quarry Press 1971), *White* (Fiddlehead Books 1972), *The Harbingers* (Quarry Press 1984), and *Visible Visions: The Selected Poems of Douglas Barbour* (NeWest Press 1984).

He is also the author of a critical study, *Worlds Out of Words: The SF Novels of Samuel R. Delany* (Bran's Head Books 1979). Parts of "these for those from whom" have appeared in *Quarry* and *Velocities.*

these for those from whom

a series of poems engendered in that textual space where certain image
systems of one Canadian poet intersect certain image systems of one
SF & F writer

Douglas
Barbour

I. J O H N   N E W L O V E   &   U R S U L A   K   L E   G U I N

meadow larks

the tree hates no one
as it sifts dimensions

    there/
        now
   here/
       then

tree translating **tree**
these shifting distances   &

melody

leaves whisper   or
the voices of blackthroats

I would be as
that tree   listening

not that one

the chrome crumpling   noise
too much   the face

shocked flat

of that death

refused   (*refused*)

yet no hatred   yet

Winter descending   always   *Douglas*
now/   i seek   *Barbour*
nothing /   see
nothing as the snow
boils on the Yangtze
butterflies broken
on the starry wheel

i follow north   follow
no trail
across that country
this one   now
i don't know
when snow   or
just ice   what
where   i   began
now everywhere
this sun a
white knob on pale sky
i twist

& when discover

beyond that ridge of dark ice
crenelated   notches
the sheer fall of

time   gone
that creature

& here   o
hear me   the guns
glimmer fretfully &
yonder   against
the far off darkening night

the icy city glows tall
& cold   so cold
& bright it rises

3. D U N C A N   C A M P B E L L   S C O T T   &
R O G E R   Z E L A Z N Y

Douglas
Barbour

Dark moves
on methane snow

others move also in the stark
forest blossoming
frost   they
are alone   they
are   all   alone

are waiting
patient   their eyes
clear
above the soft fur
they have learned to wear
travelling snow
paths between
fires

now worshipped Dark
moves alone
with the light   the world
is changing   the world

is changing

4. GWENDOLYN MACEWAN & VONDA MCINTYRE

Douglas
Barbour

listen   this
shadow on black
sand   photo
synthesis   image
reversed i
will ride you
o loving darkness

into a new
light
    dark
light

5. ARCHIBALD LAMPMAN & EDWARD BRYANT

'clanking'

it rankles   a
rank smell in
the almost empty room

high towers
stooped &
keening in
steady wind
blows & blows &
blows the sand
singing within

there are these sudden
shifts of grey   or
more colorful knots of
people   passing
the time   &

there is that final
goddamn *clang*

Douglas
Barbour

the mind shutting
everything off

                    entropy

which is
to say   empty
it all out of
the eyes

he sits   now
he sits

now

6. C O L L E E N   T H I B A U D E A U   &
G O R D O N   D I C K S O N

all those worlds
strung thru space   but
theyre only a pre/text

wander among them
'at a snails pace'
eons gone
try   to remember

but history forgets
all lessons
learned so slow
they never seem to
arrive at conscious thot

its been a long time
carrying the message
thru some speedy races
evolution   & no one
sees the writing
on a clear pane of glass
snails slime clearing
in the bright glare
a window of the pentagon
perhaps   the general
stares thru   or st peters
where the pope lies
dies always in state
so far above
the small shell on the floor

& that other shell
of apocalyptic news

empty now   & still
soon to fall from
the window sill

*Douglas
Barbour*

7.   D A P H N E   M A R L A T T   &   S A M U E L   R   D E L A N Y

how the nets work

the galaxies bright meshings
fall out   far-flung
seawrack   in a trawlers
haul   in
formation

they unfold   they
enclose   they
link us   bloodpaths
& neurons

46

Douglas
Barbour

shake it   ripples   each
link tells
our civilization
is a   net?
work the possibilities
or play them

           (economics &   history   say
      what we eat out
          tonight

the small boats ploughed the sea
reaped   sweet con
fusion of desire & luck
what feeds under
ocean   under
standing   the pier casts
its shadow   too

          (or trees
    shadows
    net the light / sight
    falters in   in
    terstices of white
    & black   filigree of
    paving   sun & leaf

the connections   these
lights sign the skies with
messages   a mesh of
what 'falls from the air'
luminous map

what a japanese glass float
speaks of
bobbing among rocks near long beach
strung on a wall in montréal
other pinpoints on a map   a
cross this huge land

string them together   they
float a new imagination of

Douglas
Barbour

        (that other world   other
        nets flung by nerve
        into oxide arsenic seas

the web
weaves us all to
gether   gather
conjunctive necessity

right now   though
standing on a beach
late at night
look up
at the patterned stars
look down
        see them shine

nets   of light
language working
'the figure of outward'   inward

8. A L   P U R D Y   &   A E   V A N   V O G T

looking both ways
to the faint tracings   hung in air

        hung in air   luminous
        weaving of   aeons of
        human activity

& the empty atmosphere
of other planets   when

48

Douglas
Barbour

or here   but not now
one of us   perhaps
begins to swing
forward & back   forward
& back

     look   you can
     see them   Klee folk
     moving superimposed do
     you see   well
     feel them   sift
     imaginations dusty trails

     all those lives in
     glowing filigree
             here
     & somewhere   else
     so far   you cant
     count   nothing
     in the thin air
     of memory   meeting
           nothing

meanwhile:
the stumbling starman trips
         thru aeons trapped

behind a glass

all ways further back
& beyond   the clear helmet   stars
in strange patterns
       now forgotten
traces of cosmic
dust   now
     nothing
       waiting
         to be filled

in the dream
it was written   this way   it was
a big
bang   it was

Douglas
Barbour

                        glorious

            these excessive distances
            in time   in space

            : to be filled   with

                        a word

9. L E O N A R D   C O H E N   &   T H O M A S   M   D I S C H

a clever corpse is catching
angels

(not those in angles whirled

                        in ward & apart
                        from the everwidening ring of song

                they are very small   & they dance
                forever on a multitude of pins)

but those others   dancing
elsewhere
who whisper melodies:

            this is better than sex
            the empty wasted body knows nothing

            not what its really *like*

                        like swimming in grand marnier
                                that delicious

Douglas
Barbour

like fucking forever
            that far gone
            into flesh
            & out the other side

(escaped   left behind
now we fly
a musical scale beyond human imagination)

lyric   lying

in my bed alone   again
now i dream   of angels

counts among his influences sputnik, drop drills, Dostoevsky, *Forbid-
den Planet*, Henry Miller, Colin Wilson, bad presidents, Berkeley in the
sixties, left-handedness, classic illustrated comic books. His own books:
Jackbird (Berkeley Poets' Workshop & Press 1976), *She Comes When
You're Leaving* (Berkeley Poets' Workshop & Press 1982), *All the Clocks
Are Melting* (Velocities 1984), *Alchemical Texts* (Ocean View Books
1985), *Nuclear Futures* (Velocities 1987) and *The Bruce Boston Om-
nibus* (Ocean View Books 1987). The poems gathered here are all new
for *POLY*.

Boston has won a Pushcart Prize for fiction and the Rhysling Award for
science fiction poetry, as well as Yaddo Colony and Milford Science Fic-
tion fellowships. He has served as an editor of *Occident*, *The Open Cell*,
City Miner Magazine, and the *Berkeley Poet's Cooperative Magazine*.
His writing has appeared in *Isaac Asimov's Science Fiction Magazine*,
The New York Times Magazine, *The Twilight Zone*, *Doubleday's 100
Great Fantasy Short Stories*, and *Burning With a Vision*.

Bruce
Boston

In nights of fierce delusion
and sadistic glory
we embraced the geographic
accident of birth
as if history's abattoir
defined a godscape descended.

In days of bears and eagles
we projected our maps
at a cosmological pace,
we wired the falling sky
with instruments of terror,
the hemispheres with hate.

When demagogues create
the dawn and words
are gloved by leather,
when silos separate
and devil trees bloom
in the sun's first splinter,

the art of flight is lost,
the borders are teeming:
beyond the furious clouds
there is no longer
a curious ear pressed
upon the stars' sure static.

JumpShift/AgriStat IV/2048 Sidereal

In the chambered nautilus
of a decaying orbit,
with the liquid acceleration
of tiny butterflies
along my stranded veins,
orchestras of artillery
unmoor our homescape
from its slackened tether.

Ah the lean telemetry
and calculated yearning
of the adamantine impulse
as it primes and propels
our tumbling hemisphere
in waves which splay
the sky grasses flat.

When silver plums fall
past lives unsettled
in the sudden violence
of seasons borne awry,
I am quartered to earth
in mock crucifixion
by the whine dark rush
of velocity's climb.

*Bruce
Boston*

Bruce
Boston

When silver plums fall
in anachronous time
and noon is noon again
in the nocturnal remission
of an eastering sun,
our envelope of air
stutters with leaves.

O how the plates
and stanchions vibrate
to the quickening strain,
how the rivulets flood
our concave terrain
as we are flung to apogee
by the coda's roar.

In a chambered nautilus
taut upon its line,
the finely drifted snow
of an artificial winter
blankets the fires,
obscures the dislocations
of unnatural disaster.

In night beyond our night
the silver plums fall,
and rise against the vacuum.

Bruce
Boston

Time and again
I have known the moment
that is ever spawned
in the onrushing change
of dark to dawn

and down again.
I have seen it light
upon the breakers
and dash against the sky.
I have watched it curl

along the dunes,
elongate and limpid,
slippery as a skin of oil.
As petals flare
against the foliage

and the sea cliffs
rise about me,
tier upon staggered tier
studded with greenery,
a vertical prairie

of succulents
living from the rock itself,
how the seconds tremble,
how the light
runs to slaughter

in the swerve and bend
of gravity's calling,
how the star-streaked waves
contain the night
and all of space beyond.

after William Carlos Williams

Bruce
Boston

I will teach you my Earth people
how to perform a star flight
for you have it over a troop
of astronauts—
unless one should scour the system—
you have the space sense necessary.

See! imagination leads.
I begin with a design for a ship.
For Sol's sake not streamlined—
not silver either—and not polished!
Let it be weathered and familiar,
as full of natural color
as the world it leaves behind.

And let us have glass on all sides!
Yes windows, my Earth people!
To what purpose? So we might
see the stars streak in the wake
of our light-speed passage,
so we might watch our past shrink
and our future swell before us.

        No plastics please—
and if there must be steel
for Clarke's sake keep it covered.
Fill the corridors with earth
which gives beneath our feet,
where grass can begin to grow.
Plaster the walls and panels
with murals of your own making
or common mementos from the past,
a favorite poem or photograph—
an old poster—a dried flower—
you know the things I mean
my Earth people.

Better still, no corridors at all,
no cramped cabins to fold us in—
rather a vast and open space,
spun for gravity, where our
thoughts may freely flow,
with a river known for its warmth,
a forest or two so we can build
homes of our own choice.

Bruce
Boston

A rough and natural ship then,
a miniature Earth, still clean—
green and blue and full of clouds
if you can imagine such a thing—
and for light no glowing tubes
that turn the skin a sickly hue,
but the passing stars themselves—
magnified by sufficient art and craft
to rival the lumens of our sun.

As to the bridge and crew—
bring them down—bring them down!
A navigator, perhaps, to help
plot our course between systems,
but no communications officer
to turn our varied voices into one,
no strutting captain-king
leading us through the cosmos,
calling our ship his ship.

Let the controls remain simple.
For what reason? So any man
or woman can learn to master them,
so every one of us might take a turn
at the board and have a hand
in making our destination.

60

Bruce
Boston

And finally, each sidereal cycle,
let us sit openly with one another,
side by side beneath the trees—
my Earth people—as we conspire
to save the best in our origins
and leave the worst behind—
you have nothing to lose—
believe me, the stars
will fill your pockets.

Go ahead now
I think you are ready for flight.

science fiction classic *Moderan*, David Gerrold wrote, "the book is a mind-shattering experience. Moderan is a mechanized, robot world, a frightening place where machines act like men pretend they don't. Bunch does things with words. He does things to words. He is angering, annoying, and pyrotechnic. He is also one of the best writers of speculative fiction around."

Bunch lives and writes in St. Louis. His stories and poems have appeared in many magazines, including *New Mexico Quarterly*, *San Francisco Review*, and *Poetry Digest*. He is the only writer to be represented with two stories in Harlan Ellison's landmark *Dangerous Visions* (1967). "The Heartacher and the Warehouseman," new for *POLY*, is set in Moderan.

THE HEARTACHER AND THE WAREHOUSEMAN

David R.
Bunch

It was high on old Re-Do Row, that big Moderan warehousing
fix-strip, where this little cringe-guy walked by with his heart
in a metal carry-sack, a regular Moderan tote-poke:
and a lead from a hole in his chest trailed down
to connect to his heart in the bag—oh! STRANGE—weird thing!
(But this was Moderan, hey! where ALL people are metal-and-
people [peoples?] [metals?] [peotals?] who take pride in their ever-last
parts; where men are mostly new-processes steel now and everyone
thinks like a fort—tough, warheads firing, just-try-me! NOW! I'm rough!)
Yet—somewhere—and surely—this one had passed through a fire,
of sorts, that had quite cooked away all jollity, all mirth, all "life,"
from a face where the smile gadgets now just did not work.
However, and nevertheless, a grim kind of try and a "gameness forever"
was set in that face and you knew, YES, KNEW! that this man's moves
would never, in all his days, be for give-up-and-quitting. "MISTER
    WAREHOUSEMAN!"

I peered down Evaluator peep-grooves out through new-steel's best
    Moderan walls;
I thumbed all scans up to HIGH-SCAN-ON-SCAN, using SCAN-RAY-SCAN
    (the best);
I set the metal stocktakers to doing it!
You can believe that I looked this One quite QUITE over!
(A man with his heart in a bag?! a metal Moderan carry-poke!?)
But he was clean-on-CLEAN; no weapons bristled;
no sneaky-devices showed hidden, either (not that I could
tell). So I let him in: just hauled the big orange-half doors back
into their wall-wells. "Yes?" I glowered, cold *phfluggee-phflaggee*
voice talking. Now, just for an instant, he trembled and I knew,
yes, realized how he must be feeling just then, here at last
(after HOW many HARD years of travel?) stark-finally
before the HIGH WAREHOUSEMAN of all wide Moderan—big-ONE,
    COLD-dude,
BIGGEST-brother!—in charge of ALL parts checkouts, and especially metal
    spare hearts—ME.
(You see, I haven't always been Moderan steel, either. I feel. I
    understand. And I

CARE for others.) (A little.) "MISTER—mister WAREHOUSEMAN!" The
   trembling
was over, and a man, mission-seized, stood before me. Cold-on
the eyes struck-in; the metal hands doubled and beat rage down
hard on a place where a heart sat deep in a sack, with a lead
going straight into a hole in a chest—weird, oh, WEIRD—WEEEOOo!

David R.
Bunch

"MISTER WAREHOUSEMAN! our country has no heart!
I HAVE NO HEART—YOU HAVE NO HEART,
and YOU, the keeper of hearts—YOU!—
ARE a warehouseman!" He cast that last
just sort of out there to dingle-a-dangle—hard, hard line,
shrieked loose in the jet scream. (Yes, in my job,
the NUT always stops here.) "Well, now,"
I said, carefully selecting my speech nog-toggers
through tibs on my talk *phfluggee-phflaggee*,
"let us sort-it, NOW, look through!" And I half-twitched
a metal indicatory shoulder nodward toward
wide-and-deep "pump bins" where a whole big new
load of fresh metal hearts reposed and glowed,
just day before yesterday delivered from that zone
where they made them: Hearts 'n' Parts. "What,"
I asked, again carefully selecting the speech nog-toggers,
"kind of a heart might you be seeking—and needing—TODAY—hey,
   mister?"

"A heart! a heart!! a Heart!!! A HEART!!!!"
(Oh, he was SCREAMING)
"REAL!! heart. And NOT a can. I HAVE a can! MISTER
WAREHOUSEMAN." I saw how it could go nasty.
I rang for the guard devices and they very
effectively came on their steel tracks from those places
where they nestled as bulges in walls until such times
as I might need them to help with NUTS
out of hand. Quickly they ringed me, steel man after steel man.
Safer I felt then; so I said, hard, my sternest talk-toggers
strong-on for loud-sounds: "HELL'S BELLS, MAN, THIS IS MODERAN!
GET WITH IT, MAN! SELECT A HEART, OR SCRAM. CHOOSE ONE,
OR HIT THE ROLL-GOS, BUM!" (WELL—I couldn't
fool around. He was unnecessarily taking up

David R.
Bunch

my time. He was BOTHERING me.) I had parts to
sort and things to catalogue. There well might be
a new shipment of metal windpipes today, or maybe
a latest prosthesis for the metal brain drains on head pans,
due any day now. Or a new breakthrough in fingers.
Or lungs. A warehouseman's job is not an easy one. Try it
sometime! And I was the Chief. Along with all the other
parts, I! was the only One who had the newest hearts,
zinged in by whisk-lift—every week!—and all sizes ready, right there in my
    "pump bins."

He took my hint. He left. Just picked up his
pump in its tote-poke from its place on my out-flow
check-one-and-GO counter and cringed through the "leave" space.
"OUT!"—"YOU were NO help," I thought I heard him smoulder, or
    something
like that, far back over a leaving shoulder. Oh, well, some people
apparently just don't want help, I thought. I was HERE. I have
the BEST hearts anyWHERE in the whole game; he could have had
whatever his work-order called for. Some people (peotals) are just
hard to make sense of. NO? —I got busy. And yes, the new fingers
came, and parts for heads that day and fresh new-metal lungs—
Oh, it was day BIG at the warehouse. No time for BUMS.
—Nevertheless and how-come-ever?! SOMETHING deep down in the few
    flesh-strips I still own
writhed loose and troubled, CAUSED concern (I have to admit it); late-on-late
that night when things grew chill-still quiet and I lay in my slinger
bed far back in Sleep-Wing of Parts Warehouse, trying to turn-off—
pitch-black except for the blink-dims constantly monitoring and counting
the stock bins, and a call coming over and over; and I wondering where oh,
    where
he was: all night long out there somewhere, cold on the homeless plastic,
lunch-sacking his pump and still pleading, "A heart! a heart!! a Heart!!!
    A HEART!!!!"? *A heart?!*

A LITTLE GIRL'S XMAS IN MODERNIA. *Coastlines,* Autumn 1958,
  The Magazine of Fantasy and Science Fiction, January 1960,
  and in translation WEIHNACHTEN IN UTOPIA, in *Die Nacht der
  zehn Milliarden Lichter,* Germany 1967.

A GLANCE AT THE PAST. *Diversion,* April 1959.

THE FLESH-MAN FROM FAR WIDE. *Amazing,* November 1959.

WAS SHE HORRID. *Fantastic,* December 1959.

THE COMPLETE FATHER. *Fantastic,* January 1960.

STRANGE SHAPE IN THE STRONGHOLD. *Fantastic,* March 1960.

REMEMBERING. *Amazing,* April 1960.

PENANCE DAY IN MODERAN. *Amazing,* July 1960.

GETTING REGULAR. *Amazing,* August 1960.

A HUSBAND'S SHARE. *Amazing,* October 1960.

HAS ANYBODY SEEN THIS HORSEMAN?
  Shenandoah, Winter 1961

FINAL DECISION. *Amazing,* February 1961.

LAST DAY AND A NEW BEGINNING. *Renaissance,* 1962.

THE ONE FROM CAMELOT MODERAN. *Descant,* Winter, 1962.

THE WARNING. *Amazing,* November 1962.

BLACK CAT WEATHER. *Fantastic,* February 1963.

SURVIVAL PACKAGES. *Fantastic,* April 1963.

ONE FALSE STEP. *Fantastic,* May 1963.

SOMETIMES I GET SO HAPPY. *Fantastic,* August 1963.

2064 OR THEREABOUTS. (pseud. Darryl R. Groupe) *Fantastic,*
  September 1964.

REUNION. *Amazing,* February 1965.

PLAYMATE. *Fantastic,* June 1965.

THE WALKING, TALKING, I-DON'T-CARE MAN. *Amazing,* June
  1965.

THE MIRACLE OF THE FLOWERS. *The Smith/7,* October 1966.

INCIDENT IN MODERAN. *Dangerous Visions,* Harlan Ellison ed.,
  Doubleday 1967, Berkeley 1969, and translated as NUR EINE
  FEUERPAUSE in *15 Science Fiction Stories, Harlan Ellison's
  Grosse SF-Anthologie,* Germany 1969.

*A LITTLE AT ALL TIMES. *Perihelion Science Fiction,* Summer
  1969.

NO CRACKS OR SAGGING. *The Little Magazine,* Spring 1970.

A GLANCE AT THE PAST. *Fantastic*, October 1970.

MODERAN. Avon Books, May 1971.

*THE JOKE. *Fantastic*, August 1971.

David R.
Bunch

*TWO SUNS FOR THE KING. *If, Science Fiction*, April 1972.

*THE GOOD WAR. *Fantastic*, December 1972.

*IN THE LAND THAT AIMED AT FOREVER. *Fantastic*, May 1974

*AMONG THE METAL-AND-PEOPLE PEOPLE. *New Dimensions 4*,
Robert Silverberg ed., New American Library 1974.

*THE DIRTY WAR. *Future Pastimes*, anthology, Aurora 1977.

HOW THEY TOOK CARE OF SOUL IN A LAST DAY FOR A NON-
BEGINNING. (excerpt from *MODERAN*) *Umbral*, Fall 1978.

*WHEN THE METAL EATERS CAME. *Galaxy*, June/July 1979.

*A LITTLE GIRL'S SPRING DAY IN MODERAN. *Galaxy*
September/October 1979.

*DECEMBER FOR STRONGHOLD 9. *Amazing*, June 1982.

*THE HEARTACHER AND THE WAREHOUSEMAN. *POLY* 1989.

(* not collected in MODERAN)

C30 cassette *Slits in Aerosol Green* was characterized in *New Musical Express* as "half an hour of poetry from a twisted mind." Darlington has recorded with the electronics group U.V. Pop, edits *Ludds Mill* from Yorkshire in the UK, and has published his poems in *Ambit, Bogg, Gargoyle, Electronic Soundmaker*, the *Umbral Anthology of SF Poetry*, and elsewhere. Book publications include *Stopwatch* (New English Libraries 1974) and *Hard Lines* (Faber & Faber 1984).

POLY   What is interesting and significant about speculative/sur-real/science/science-fiction poetry?

Darlington   SF is a popular—non elitist—literary form, which opens up a window of access to experiment and ideas otherwise restricted to ghettos/ivory towers of academe.

THE FIGHT IN THE CAVE OF THE MOON BUTCHERS

THE MOONCALF PASTURES

Andrew

Darlington

So we poor terrestrial castaways, lost in that wild-growing moon jungle, crawled in terror before the sounds that had come upon us.

The First Men in the Moon—H.G. Wells 1901

Pteradons glide my room
each morning before dawn.
I taste the audible smile
of their scales
through the hooks
beneath my flesh.
I know such yearnings.
My hands become claws as
fluid dissolves in soft curves
through the silence
of hall and landing.
I know the instinct to simpler forms
in the low cellular echoes
aching down the spinal staircase
towards phantom primeval suns.
My room submerges, liquid,
ebbing memories of primal slime.
Flakes of time float loose
leaving salt reptile aftertaste.
In such moments, the urge
to devolve becomes real.
Through the barbs
beneath the cortex
I share their stillness.
I pace slow,
leave web tracks
in the warm mud
across the rug
while lizards
slither & coil
in the moist stink
of rich decay,
beneath all that's
rational and cold.

Moving slow.
Pared down to guiltless indolence.
They're millenia-deep
glimpsed in sharp echoes
at the pit of my eyes.
I remember the mindless reptile purity
that's now resurfacing...
And all the while,
beyond the pteradon's glide,
through the casement,
the silver ribs of mud-flats
leak away without end,
achingly soft
towards extinction

*Andrew
Darlington*

AGAINST HELIOCENTRICITY
THE HERMES TRISMEGISTUS CODEX

Andrew
Darlington

The thought's tormenting me
—Copernicus got it WRONG!
This Medieval text, this flowering script,
debates alchemical wisdoms
uninfected by infinity...

In codex ciphers it spells
worlds the SENSES know are true.

A clockwork cosmology harmonises
—the wild-haired imaginings of infinity
are grown by the de-mystified
to explain the wonder they've lost.

The thought's tormenting me
—Ptolemy was right.

The stars are holes
in this print sky,
predating all that's falsely rational.

This sky's still here,
choked in vortices of
gods, wisdoms, beliefs & religions.
They're woven in pre-heliocentric diagrams
mocking in their perfection...

... personalised solar systems,
symmetrical constellations in whirls
of animated planetary orbs.
Numinous curves of mythic complexity
spun legends of cosmic theology,
ether winds describing thumb-print eddies
in fine-line loops
in engraved spirals
that orbit prints
that have outlived centuries...

The thought's tormenting me
—how can I disbelieve such beauty?

*Andrew
Darlington*

THE WAVE-PARTICLE PARADOX
DATA FROM PARTICLE TRAPS

Andrew
Darlington

Driving through the heart of freezing suns,
cruising inverted cities hung with shape...

you know these scenes from television.

concrete and glass hung mountain-high
                right out into space,
fashion-lepers pacing the crosswalks,
innoculated into innocence
in a taxi to the particle traps...

others slink under perimeter wire
and track across mud-slick flower-beds,
into this anaemic white strip-light apron,
plate-glass doors, corridors
                    and staircases
going down to this planet's core...

you know these scenes from television

from
storms on the surface of freezing suns
to the swarming streets with
the air like liquid speed
we are here
        where eternity begins
hot-wired on accumulating momentum
innoculated into the night-time vision
of the wave-particle paradox.

I CAN'T QUITE REMEMBER THE RE-CREATION OF THE WORLD

I can't quite remember the re-creation of the world.
I remember climbing into the obsidian machine.
I can still see the faces and the glass tubes
in their neat insect tiers.
I remember the endless dunes,
the flatlands roiled purple in holocaust,
I remember the burning trees,
I remember insane people dancing, copulating
and murdering in the street,
I remember the comet splitting the sky and
letting in the multi-coloured clouds,
I remember the chanting, the breaching of the
Mayan tombs, the reciting of the cuneiform texts,
the piles of limbs in neat stacks
beside the highways, and telegraph poles
at odd predatory angles.
I can see each apocalyptical vision
as if it were yesterday
but I can't quite remember
the re-creation of the world.

Andrew Darlington

ANIMALISMS
COPERNICUS, CITY OF THE DEAD

Andrew
Darlington

Moon silver splinters adrift in flakes,
shuffle the shift of leaves,
motes swim veins of fibre,
the glowing spores of spatial vacuum.
Through the precinct, pacing pavement cracks,
packs of Supermarket Trolleys infiltrate
lean wire skeletons ghosting dead caves of glass,
predatory the hunter with starry particles,
amoebic burning in ice, in sensual warmth,
in frayed steel, as fragmented lamination syringes,
subcutaneously, she howls at each tiny penetration,
skin layered back, charcoal black, blowing like ash,
pegged out, splayed in cross at each point of
the cycle of the moon, jagged silver cells
lovingly lacerate with intimate tongues,
her blood pulsing milk, enervated with light,
illuminated until she gleams, moist with spectral ignition,
lazing with flesh dripping like sweat
and she stands in ecstasy transfigured,
a thing of cellular light naked of sin or guilt,
trolleys kneel to kiss her bleeding feet
that ebb their perfect purity into dead leaves.
In lunar whiteness irradiated she leads,
huntress of the moon...

A CONVENTION OF GHOSTS

for J.G. Ballard

... thru unfocused eyes,
a cocktail lounge filled
with storms of chaffinches,
beautifully absurd,
a molten liquidity of wings
circling a million filing cabinets
& incandescent banks of pink VDU's

winking
like orchid forests...

Andrew
Darlington

speaks with perhaps the strongest bardic voice in science fiction. A consistent contributor to the Pournelle anthologies, Dillingham otherwise publishes poetry infrequently. Despite this infrequency, it is no exaggeration to credit his influence with the shaping of much of speculative poetry's character. Over the years, he has personally encouraged a number of the contributors to *POLY*.

In 1976 as editor of *Cthulhu Calls*, he compiled *A Preliminary Bibliography of Science Fiction Poetry*—still essential reading. Some of the poems here are reprinted with permission of the author from *Treaders of Starlight*, *The Anthology of Speculative Poetry*, and *Star*Line*. The two untitled poems and "Cloud Skier" are published here for the first time.

Peter
Dillingham

Star   Star's
Black   Black
Balled   Swan
By   (Song)
Space-Time   Hatching

N A R C I S S E   A N D   T H E   B L A C K   H O L E

Having fallen to within $1.5(2GM/c^2)$
Of the black pool's center,
$Narcisse_{psi}$ reaches out,
Space-like through space
To possess a stranger,
An endless succession
Of casual passers by,

In ecstacy,
$Narcisse_n$ contemplates $Narcisse_1$,
A moment standing still forever
Transcending myth and dream,
Transcending the heavy scent,
The alien flesh of flowers,
A perfect image frozen forever
On the imperturbable surface
Of that dark mirror.

Holo-Caustic—to view—in a dark room, hold a flashlight exactly illuminating the circle and read with a magnifying glass. This adds the approximate experience of the astronomer.

Peter

Dillingham

Left Hemisphere	Right Hemisphere
	the cell reacts
"It was visible by day	a glorious
like Venus;"	sacrificial blossoming
Yang Wei-te	at 10,000 km/sec
Chief Computer of the Calendar,	phagocytic...
told the Emperor	triggered by
in July 1054;	contagion's spread
"pointed rays	a malignant thrusting forth
shot out from it	of virulent sentience
on all sides;	from long containment
the color was reddish-white..."	the cell reacts
	a glorious
In November, 1572, Tycho Brahe,	sacrificial blossoming
Astronomer of Florence,	at 10,000 km/sec
"saw,	phagocytic...
with inexpressible astonishment,	triggered by
near the zenith,	contagion's spread
in Cassiopeia,	a malignant thrusting forth
a radiant star	of virulent sentience
of extraordinary magnitude."	

COSMOLOGICAL HOLOPHRASTICS

1—The Black Hole   2—Matter Antimatter

Peter
Dillingham

1—The Black Hole	2—Matter Antimatter
Holehearted	Wholeface
Holotropic	Hollowface
Wholehog	
Whole-in-one	
Holeness	
Holiness	

EPITAPH FOR A STAR

Brief glory of your dusky spoondrift spiral,
Spendthrift giant of the blue flame of youth,
You left behind only singular chaos,
And a vortex of memory.

Antediluvians   *Peter*
Old land lords   *Dillingham*
We who turn in the clouds
Deep billowy havens
A kind of survival
Kaleidals of fugitive resonance
In vast sky palaces of icy mist
Since minds' taut linkage
Sheared flesh
The waters licking at our heels

Millenium after millenium
Without form
Without substance
Haunted by memory
Denied the stars
And despairing reincarnation
So many have departed
Seeking destruction
The dark towering nimbus
Those cthonic storm clouds
Charged with angry alien life

Or ventured earthward
The forbidden quest
Whispering fantoccini of the fog
Dreamwrights
The Possessors

Peter
Dillingham

sankdeep in the lime of her
quick in the lime of her
the sea salt salt blood soil and song of her
swelling life of her
thundering swell of her

time warps

siege my strange one
perilous
your island of appletrees
maze your masks
my beckoning fair one
eyes the glinting frost of opals
floes
crevass and glacial shadow

Pulseyes   eyes the glinting frost of opals
scintillations of symbionic sensors   teleplastic eyes
eyes a pointilistic swarming   luminaries
conjuring a species' young   infants blind at birth
cloistered   still rime feathered hollows
those fragile niduses of sentient light   awaiting visitation
...and visions of the damned   rejected hosts
harrowing those yawning orbits   inscapes without interface
mute naked singularities...
                    e 'l canto di quei lumi
Oh quanto é corto il dire

Peter
Dillingham

CLOUD SKIER

Peter
Dillingham

Alone,
Without world or woman,
Weight of flesh, word,
That weariness,
The skier skiis the clouds.

Aloof,
He swoops
Down tufts of cirrus,
Springs and soars—vorlage;
Then strides, kick and glide,
Across vast sky fields of stratus.

Serene,
He serpentines
Down deep powder slopes,
Tumultuous heapings of cumulus...
O so swift and free
My spirit schusses.

Sojourner among the Nephele   exultations of cloud   *Peter*
those étages of sentient mist   masters of flying white   *Dillingham*
cloud poems   allusive as Li Shang-yin's Patterned Lute

Ecstacy of Incus

    1 ⌒
    2 △
    1 ⌒
    2 △
    3 ▲
    1 ⌒
    2 △   *Excelsiors of Cirrus*
    3 ▲
    2 △   4 ⋋
    3 ▲   0
                                    4 ⋋
    2 △   0
    3 ▲   4 ⋋
    9 ▤   1 ⌣
    3 ▲   4 ⋋
    9 ▤   1 ⌣
                                    4 ⋋
                                    1 ⌣

                                    4 ⋋
                                    0
                                    4 ⋋
                                    0
                                    4 ⋋

Possessed   yet forever barbarian
mere courier of ciphers

                                                              I depart

well known for his fiction, has also published books of poetry including *Highway Sandwiches* (with Marilyn Hacker, 1970), *The Right Way to Figure Plumbing* (Basilisk Press 1972), *Haikus of a Pillow* (Belleview Press 1980), *ABCDEFG HIJKLM NPOQRST UVWXYZ* (Anvil Press 1981), and *Orders of the Retina* (Toothpaste Press 1982). His poems have appeared in *Harper's*, *Velocities*, *The Paris Review*, *The Times Literary Supplement*, and *Poetry*. Disch lives in New York City.

Of Tom Disch's verse essays in *Burn This* (Hutchinson 1982), *Newsweek* book critic and *POLY* contributor David Lehman writes, "[they] appeal to that line of writers from Pope to Auden and John Hollander who value urbanity, strike a balance between plain address and epigrammatic poise, and consider criticism as far too important to be left entirely to critics." Disch and Lehman are also represented in the *Communicating Vessels* section of *POLY*, as collaborators. *Richard Andsoforth*, subtitled *A Forgery*, was written at the invitation of the Australian Broadcasting Company. This is its first appearance in print.

RICHARD ANDSOFORTH

A Forgery

Tom
Disch

SCENE i, SOME RAMPARTS

Mnemonius
Let me, Kleptomander, while still it's night,
Ask you this then: do you believe in God?

Kleptomander
God! *I,* believe in God? who serve a king
So steeped in blood as he, Abraxion?
God? *You* ask me that, Mnemonius?
You, who but two hours since have lit your wick
At the same sweet tickling flames? You can ask that?

Mnemonius
Aye, I ask you, as a friend, and as
Another bored watchman set upon these heights,
With nothing but this little lane of stars
Between the pines to light our discourse. I
Ask you, in good faith, if you believe in God.

Kleptomander
And I reply, in any faith you like,
No. Gods are for fools and woman; I
Am neither. I am my own man, and the King's
Who pays my wage and lets me strut upon
The stage we have tonight disaudienced
So vilely. Don't you love a good outrage?

Mnemonius
You're right, I suppose, but I could wish we'd shipped
With other kings to other shores.

Kleptomander
                    And dipped
Our wicks in other oils? And flamed less bright?
Mnemonius, we were like gods tonight
Ourselves. The land we've conquered lies before us
Like whores who'll say, sincerely, they adore us
When once our knives are at their throats. But hark,
Who's there?

Tom
Disch

[*Abraxion enters.*]

Abraxion
                    'Tis I, Abraxion, your king.
It's well you saw me two sword-lengths before
You would have forfeited your pay. Have there
Been ghosts, or other disturbances, to entertain
your watch.

Mnemonius
                    My lord, if laxity there's been,
It's mine, for I, in my midnight idleness,
Distracted him with schoolboy riddles.

Abraxion
                                        As?
Ask me, for I've a wit as sharp a steel.
Show me whatever knotted thought, I'll deal
With it as it were cheese.

Mnemonius
                    Do you believe . . .

Abraxion
In what?

Kleptomander
                    In men's right, my lord, to live
As we have lived tonight—and hope to still,
By your permission and most gracious will.

Mnemonius
In God!

Abraxion
            (Now here's a man who speaks his thoughts!)
Are you as loyal as you're candid? Speak!

Mnemonius
My lord, I've sworn to serve you, and my hands
Still reek. What would you have me say? I'm yours
Again—when I have had four hours sleep,
A change of clothes, some wine, and my back-pay.

Abraxion
What is this miscreant's name?

Kleptomander
                    Mnemonius.

Abraxion
Mnemonius, come, you'll join my bodyguard.

Mnemonius
My Lord!

Kleptomander
        Good God!

Abraxion
                Mnemonius, obey!

Abraxion   [*alone*]

Tom
Disch

Soon comes the miserable morning after,
The women weeping at the chicken roosts,
The virgins disinterred by vengeful kin,
The flagging energies, and sense of sin.
But first, let me enjoy this reign that's mine
By right, and let me yet, while still it's night,
Imagine laws of governance, as thus:

The man who contradicts me dies at dawn!
No, that's too much. Some men there are oppose
As whores may tease, to make us hungrier
For their predestinate tongues up our ass.
Another law then. This: all men must kiss
Something they loathe, some mawkish crucifix
They'll call a god. I'll have them pray to it
In church, o' Sunday, when they're in their freshest
Uniforms, and those who best abase
Themselves I'll decorate with buttons gilt
With the gold-capped molars of men they've killed.
Why, what a state I'll make, and what a hero
I! They'll say of me, 'The man's a Nero!
A Ghenghis Khan! A monster! But—a king!'
And when I snap my fingers, they'll do anything.

SCENE iii, A CHAMBER

Ann
Woe's me, Amanda, and you would feel the same
If you had any sense of decency
Or shame!

Tom
Disch

Amanda

　　　My lady, I've five blood-stained sheets
To wash, as many notes of sympathy
To draft, and when they're signed, I must rehearse
Assorted orphans for the requiem mass
At which they are to sing. What I must feel
I'll feel tomorrow with a private grief.

　　　　　　　　　　　　　　　　[Amanda exits]

Ann　*[alone]*
I'd kill myself, as other women in
My shoes have done, and I could name them, too.
But what's the use? The only victory
Is to outlive our predators, and I,
A victim born, need not a victim die.
I'll marry him, and live, and breed, and turn
His children into enemies, and laugh
At ballads sung of parricide and war.
I'll waste his wealth and dress myself in furs
And jewels so rare I'll be his treasurer's
Despair. These very shoes in which I might
Be buried, if I killed myself tonight,
I'll dance in on his tomb, and give them, in
My will, to a daughter with an equal skill.

SCENE iv, ANN'S FUNERAL

Abraxion
There goes a head I might regret. And yet . . .

Mnemonius
And yet and yet and yet. We must not let
Mere preference get in the way of need.
The state you rule is like a restless steed;
It must be curbed. (And Ann's been curbed indeed.)

Abraxion

And yet . . . Excuse me, I am not myself.

What wars are planned? what plunder, pillage, pelf?

Tom

Disch

Mnemonius

We mean to place a tax upon dartboards,

Tennis, wine, and song.

Abraxion

What else is new!

Mnemonius

The deaths of Nero! Ghenghis Khan! And you!

Here, tyrant!

[*Stabs Abraxion.*]

Here's the tax most overdue:

Here's death, and death, and death, and death for you!

[*Abraxion dies.*]

E P I L O G U E

Mnemonius   [*alone*]

Now I, may be, am king, but keep your seat,

For vengeance comes, and, God knows, it is sweet.

But while I'm king, let me say this: a king

Has got an ass to kiss, and here is mine.

Kiss it, groundlings, by my Right Divine!

But soft, I see assassins entering,

And they are mine.

[*Assassins enter and stab Mnemonius, who dies.*]

T H E   E N D

lives and writes in Oakland, California. A film critic, he is the author of "Notes on Hans Christian Anderson & the Oedipus Complex" (*Journal of Popular Film* 1975), "Doubleness in Hitchcock: Seeing the Family Plot" (*Bright Lights* 1978) and "Woody Allen's Love Letter to Diane Keaton" (*Bright Lights* 1980). His poems and works of literary criticism have appeared in *Beloit Poetry Journal*, *ELH*, and *Open Letter*. His pieces for *POLY* are new. A sample of his thoughts on poetry of the kind inhabiting this collection:

POLY   What is interesting and significant about your writing, and about speculative/surreal/science/science-fiction poetry?

Foley   The joy and pleasure of speech. I want to juxtapose the opening of Breton's Nadja:

> Who am I? If this once I were to rely on a proverb than perhaps everything would amount to knowing whom I "haunt." I must admit that this last word is misleading, tending to establish between certain beings and myself relations that are stranger, more inescapable, more disturbing than I intended. Such a word means much more than it says, makes me, still alive, play a ghostly part, evidently referring to what I must have ceased to be in order to be *who* I am. Hardly distorted in this sense, the word suggests that what I regard as the objective, more or less deliberate manifestations of my existence are merely the premises, within the limits of this existence, of an activity whose true extent is quite unknown to me.

with a few passages from Samuel R. Delany's *The Jewel-Hinged Jaw*:

> Any serious discussion of speculative fiction must first get away from the distracting concept of s-f content and examine precisely what sort of word-beast sits before us.

Jack
Foley

I can think of no series of words that could appear in a piece of naturalistic fiction that could not also appear in speculative fiction. I can, however, think of many series of words that, while fine for speculative fiction, would be meaningless as naturalism. Which then is the major and which the subcategory?

Consider: naturalistic fictions are parallel-world stories in which the divergence from the real is too slight for historical verification.

POLY   Why are you interested in writing about movies?

Foley   I am not at all interested in "reviewing," in telling people which movies are good or bad. What I am interested in is *finding out what I'm doing there in the dark.* This is true of my poetry also.

It was extraordinary how easily he fell. I had expected something more spectacular. The arms raised in protest. A cry.

Jack
Foley

All details have been eliminated and the foliage of the trees reduced to a minimum to reveal the geometric severity of the houses.

How easy it was to trap him in my sights, how easy to pull the trigger.

To die means to be no longer in the world.

How easy it was to trap him in my sights, how easy to pull the trigger. To die means to be no longer in the world. There is something here which will not declare itself. His eyes were large and trusting. He did not cry out. There is something perhaps in the nature of the subject.

The reason that fortune is said to be friendly to young men is that they choose their lot in life from among those arts and professions that flourish in their youth; but as the world by its nature changes in taste from year to year, they later find themselves in their old age strong in such wisdom as no longer pleases and therefore no longer profits. Thus there came about a great and sudden revolution in literary affairs in Naples.

A few moments before she died her arms flew out suddenly in front of her. She rose up in the bed. Silently, and with her eyes shut, her hands whirled violently in the air. These are the cogitations of a sky, graying and silent, in which the morning's objects stand in an unfamiliar light.

I stood, quiet among the trees, my rifle, poised,

Jack
Foley

He stood, roughly, in the doorway, eating an apple.
She immediately absented herself from the room.

His teeth told much of his story. There was something far more frequent
about the way he ate than was possible for a stranger. She returned. She
stood now in the center of the room. Come in won't you, she said. In the
doorway the light from outside entered the room. He moved to the center of
the room, passing between the light and the woman. She asked, Had he
had a pleasant journey. With the door closed the room was considerably
darker than before. She asked, Would you like me to open the shade? Sitting
down on the couch he answered that it would not be necessary. Pain is a
frequent visitor to the mind but it is rarely welcome. I am alone. She began
to pace. The light at the edges of the shades was bright but the room was
dark. He had finished his apple. She began to unbutton her blouse. The
brassiere beneath it was gray with use. I do not know the name of that. I am
uncertain as to what that is called.

for James Broughton

Who has told you this? Where do your messages come from?   *Jack*
                                                                            Foley

He entered the room slowly, carefully. Each position, he thought, has its
occult potency. As they waited—and watched—in the waiting room each
person assumed a different, and changing, attitude.

What do I see as I sit and look, here and elsewhere? Noise of traffic?
Skateboard on the cement? An automobile shifts gears? There is something
interesting in my landscape, even the grayness of a concrete "yard." I come
face to face, again and again, with what I do not know. Do know.

She stood before him. He touched her face, sadly. I meant gladly. She said,
I had hoped to see you again but the day was ending. She touched him,
lightly, upon the arm. He remembered her from several years before. He
wished nothing from her. He wished something from her. As he touched her
he remembered. These are the landscapes she said, showing him. He had
no wish to go. He wished to go. Her landscapes filled the room. How do
you know whether a painting is good or bad? she asked him. How can you
tell, when you have finished a painting, whether you have realized the
intentions you began with? During the course of a painting, intentions may
have come and gone... She touched him again. As she spoke the day was
changing. With infinite care and attention he noticed every gradation and
shift of the light upon her. She stood now in partial darkness. I have been
alive for over forty years, he said, there are good days and bad days, the
light which touches you touches everything.

from LETTERS: COLLAGE POEMS

Jack
Foley

THE WORLD IS EVERYTHING THAT IS THE
CASE. THOUGHT CAN BE OF WHAT IS NOT
THE CASE.

the favored victim   the sweetings the boundary
the scuff
to allow the specially plaited grass bag

refuse to divulge
the world or the bear be called to allow the spirits these media will come
I will reckon him

the esteem in which   in new territory
which others may find too Christian
the likelihood that the village

you were a public return had no connection all in vain
more one or the other
very thick and large

we talked of a part of the craving the fullest satisfaction
I am immediately nervous
week stretch

I have likened to the note of a gong
            when he kills

makarios in malta   *Jack*
his winter in his buff the next flow of material to well up through the split   *Foley*
the age of reptilian magic
the regularity of the ocean floor enveloped in fog & clouds here are waters &
    fire
our vegetation is an artificial assemblage of ancient origins
produced by turbidity currents of a kind that could
charlie's figures for the loss of sunlight in London
it was all done   possibilities least leap alive
a guide to the natives   a guide to ciaucoatl
    here is seen the divinity bending above & below him the dancer
on the imperfect right side
a bill of complaint   a mountain of water might be read
    for the various yearly festivals
(xiuhtilmatli) which is woven in openwork and trimmed with a red border of
    eyes
to recognize in the number 18 a number pertaining to a deity
20 day periods which make the year day
    the meaning of cimi is death
in the act of grasping, as in the character for the east, where the hand (as it
    were) draws up the sun

the Aztec name for the day
of the upper right-hand corner of 31a
is entirely destroyed
lord of the second north period
image of the sun   widespread notion   a speaker, a tlatoani
struck by a speak on the jaguar skin also a jag
I think this can only mean there is no reference here
the number of the week day the day sign
Zaana means "to give birth," "to beget" & Xaana, chaana, creatrix, of men
    & of fishes

Jack
Foley   the time began slowly to penetrate him
                                              the days fell awake
                    the Morning Star the Evening Star the pebble became the earth
                    on each side the waters
                                        as he lingered
                    baby swimming down the river   used in the psalmes
                    or that the gifts of the body are better than those of the mind
                            wreak pleasure, wreak hatred

...with a nightmare face

         foreheadless & chinless

from the brow ridges

           in a level line

juts out like the beak of a bird

             the septum of the nose

a complicated tatu in green ink

principal sites greatly post-dated those of the old

    possesses histories

perforce unsettled   fattened on maize are newly fed

    a dish to beat

       were they the degeneration from

stands with the sacrificial knife

           forcibly united

dated inscriptions cease to be carved

     lamps to the likeness of a faintly-glowing macaw

    they do not know how many days

from a sweaty face, then the body rolled down

ceremonial domestication

what happened to the potato

     seed planting of aboriginal

a lot of our native crops

       asserted that vision comes from the rays

           of the eyes

     capture, nursing by a foster mother

rightly towards us

but I don't want you

to think

   I have ever seen

  once every month he used to take some

Latcham in Santiago, who, I found

   "The Golden Bough"

when Xenothon celebrated the return to his country he made

great offerings of swine

         many times the size those of sorghums

the wild forms live in the mountains well above

Jack
Foley

READING: *THE*
INDIANS' BOOK

108

Jack

Foley

Isthmus of Panama
culturally there are a number
what seas what shores what grey rocks and what islands
many indecorums in other parts
obstinate peevish willful self-conceited
come closer again
he heth consumed a whole night in lying
raigne, especially
he enjoy a bell for mass
to the Morning Star she gave him all that she had
in quick dance time while the whistle & drum are sounded
the Power of Flint from the Morning Star
the Power of the Storm
the lion also confirms the attribution
a few human beings have as yet traveled
songs of war/hunting songs/barter songs
songs to cure the sick/corn/grinding songs
hand game songs/cradle songs/holy or
"medicine"/songs
league fell apart

1980 winner of the Rhysling Award for the best short poem in science fiction, has edited *The Magazine of Speculative Poetry*, *Star* * *Line*, and the Owlswick anthology *Burning With a Vision*. His books of poems are *Peregrine* (Salt-Works Press 1978), *A Measure of Calm* (with Andrew Joron, Ocean View Books 1985), *Perception Barriers* (Berkeley Poet's Workshop & Press 1987) and *Co-Orbital Moons* (Ocean View Books 1987).

Frazier lives in Nantucket, describes himself as a science poet, and is a frequent contributor to *Isaac Asimov's Science Fiction Magazine*. His poems have also appeared in *Fantasy & Science Fiction*, *Amazing Stories*, and in *Songs From Unsung Worlds* (ed. Bonnie Bilyeu Gordon) and *Light Years and Dark* (ed. Michael Bishop). "Three Scientific Love Poems" constitute three-fifths of a poem-cycle. A fourth poem of the cycle, *Co-Orbital Moons*, appeared in *Velocities* in 1984, and was reprinted in the Ocean View Books collection of that name. The last has yet to appear.

THREE SCIENTIFIC LOVE POEMS

ANATOMICAL TRANSPARENCIES

Robert
Frazier

When the skin is stripped off our arguments
even ones small and scientific
they glisten with color inside
photomicrographs and frog diagrams
oscilloscopic reptiles sidewinding
across the Saharas of our hearts
when we unveil more layers
like transparencies
overlaid in a biology book
serial as laundry hung to dry
clothespinned to our timeline
then we see the guts of them tangled
and convoluted as brains
with facts and frictions webbing
their plumb frames like ganglia

At your clearest cross-section
your nervous system wavers
air streaming above a baking pavement
and then ignites with anger
and bundles glow like optic fibers

As mine the veins and arteries ramble
in the twisted signatures of tornadoes
where guilt is carved
in graphs and modern petroglyphs
across the level plains of my chest

When I turn our diagrams together
the levels are sealed with static
which crackles when unzipped
forming momentary blue arcs like those
inferences threading our parts of speech

When your hand reaches across the light
years touching me to make amends
the contact has a scent of enigma
thick as the cloud of electrons
buzzing around a heavy atom

Robert
Frazier

FISSIONARY DREAMS

Once I made a nocturnal breakthrough
as an expedition to the inner wilderness of cells

Beyond the ceaseless testing of each specimen
beneath the dense canopy of feeling

Beyond the laboratory jungle of love
where water boas can swallow you whole

And the research grants must be stalked by those
with bites bigger than an average alligator

I can still dream and redream that time
to remember the sudden right feeling

Upon waking with that image that amalgam
of faces burned into my skull cavity

Like a forest fire scarring
totally around the base of a mountain

Back then my mind was a microscope
with no reticular eyepiece

So that each new infatuation was held
unique to its own scales of comparison

114   Isolated as a cavefish adrift
             in the pools of its own blindness

Robert   One year the centrifuge haunted my sleep
Frazier   then the vines of beakers and tubing

             Even my dreams turned glassine
             until that final night I tossed feverishly

             And all specific knowledges drained
             down eddies of magnification

             And atoms suspended like asteroids in orbit
             grew molten to my fantasies

             And mysteries unfolded full blown
             from the glassblower's rod

             As shining as a benzene ring
             a minute circle of light

             Now you know why I sometimes rub my eyes
             when we're in bed with lamps out

             Why the rods and cones in colored excitement
             begin the dream again

             The shattering heat which destroyed
             my narrow and linear theorems

             About the architecture of pheromones
             and the lives that dance

             maniacal and moonstruck as puppets
             on their molecular strings

Unhinge the petals of your numbers
in slumber where you lie
race tonight
give up your random light
scattering every which way
chase me right out to the fringes
of the magnetic envelope
let me feast in binges
ignite my pores with white
noise and brownian mountains
fountains of self-replicant flakes
dope me until we're slaked
numb with numerals and lust
then trust
me give me sway
we'll twine
my contour to your shape
drape your curvature on mine
again elope with jugs of fractal wine

Robert
Frazier

BEYOND THE MICHELSON/MORLEY EXPERIMENT

Robert
Frazier

—3000 Å—

Ether drift enigma
absolute motion
variable mass

—4000 Å—

These factors beamed through
the researchers like the sun
itself split apart by a prism

—5000 Å—

Null results defied experimental
reason until an idea bloomed:
the cosmos wasn't built on ether

—6000 Å—

Methods of precision became
Albert Michelson's genius
and an ongoing obsession

—7000 Å—

The fixed velocity of light
a yardstick to endure
But never improve

—8000 Å—

The importance of fractals lies in their ability to capture the essential
features of very complicated and irregular objects and processes, in a way
that is susceptible to mathematical analysis.

Robert

Frazier

Benoit Mandelbrot

They said, "You have a blue guitar,
You do not play things as they are."
The man replied, "Things as they are
Are changed upon the blue guitar."

Wallace Stevens

The crystalline structures step,
    soldiers in perfect rule,
    down to the vanishing point
    of any metallic molecule:
self-similar—an ordered poise.

The snowflake processes imitate,
with every falling whole,
a diffused, mirrored forest
of every branch and bole:
self-cloning—this white noise.

The snowflake processes imitate,
    with every falling whole,
    a diffused, mirrored forest
    of every branch and bole:
self-cloning—this white noise.

The crystalline structures step,
soldiers in perfect rule,
down to the vanishing point
of any metallic molecule:
self-similar—an ordered poise.

conducted the following conversation, "Ambitious to Wake Up," under ideal circumstances: by mail over several months, with ample leisure for reflection and no long silences "on the tape." The setting of this conversation may therefore be conjured in pure imagination. Somewhere airless, distant, and clear, in another life, or to borrow from the Tom Disch play in *POLY*, simply on "some ramparts."

One of the two voices, Gene Van Troyer, is introduced elsewhere in *POLY* in conjunction with his long poem "The Myth of the Man at the Center." Under his pen, or rather, his computer, the resulting conversation sometimes resembles a catalog of possibilities for poetry, as interesting for what is left-out as for what is included. There is much here to stir, stimulate, and even to offend the complacent.

The owner of the other disembodied voice, poet William Stafford, has lived in a mode most uncomplacent. A conscientious objector in World War II and active in the pacifist movement, he lives in Oregon. Among his many books of poems are *Travelling Through the Dark* (Harper & Row 1962), *Stories That Could Be True: New and Collected Poems* (Harper & Row 1977), and *Poems for Tennessee* (with Robert Bly and William Matthews 1971). His reading has been recorded on a Folkways record album, *Today's Poets 2* (1968).

His work has earned him Yaddo Foundation and Guggenheim Fellowships, the Union League Civic and Arts Foundation Prize of *Poetry, Chicago* (1959), the Melville Cane Award (1974), and the National Book Award (1963). Stafford has also served as Consultant in Poetry to the Library of Congress. His thoughts on speculative poetry should be of certain interest.

AMBITIOUS TO WAKE UP

A conversation between William Stafford and Gene Van Troyer

Stafford
Van Troyer

GVT   *Something you said a while back intrigued me. I had asked you for a few poems for* Star*Line, *explaining what the magazine was like, and describing the Science Fiction Poetry Association. You sent me three poems and replied that the idea of the SFPA "energized and excited" you, and that you had always felt your poetry was reaching for an area akin to the Science Fiction Ideal. I'm wondering why you felt that way.*

WS   Part of my excitement came just from learning that not fiction only, but poetry, might have a place and find readers amongst those who enjoy the space and freedom that are a part of s-f. I glimpsed an outlet for works that combine poetry and that larger world. Glimpsing that outlet, I felt ambitious to wake up some of my writing to enter that area.

GVT   *What is there in s-f that gives you the sense that your poetry has been reaching for the s-f ideal? Or perhaps I should say, What is there in your poetry that gives you this sense?*

WS   Whenever you can experiment with thought, conversation, or writing in such a way as to lift off fast and far without the need to take care of weight, expense, and other workaday responsibilities, you can adventure more. I've always felt that poetry has that lightness or speed or range. Further, many of the ideas that come to me in writing poetry bounce off advances in speculation and knowledge that derive from science. I find the combination of elements that are prevalent in s-f to be natural to my way of going in poetry.

GVT   *Do you recall when it was that you first began writing poems with specifically s-f themes?*

WS   It's hard for me to go back far enough to run out of possible s-f themes in my writings. When I was in grade school my father bought me H.G. Wells's *Outline of History* (several volumes, as I remember), and the same appetite that made me race through accounts of Early Man and exotic places led me to sift onward through other of Wells's works and other works with that flavor. I think those flavors haunted my earliest writings.

GVT   *Is the ''s-f ideal'' a more-or-less recent direction in which some of your poetry is moving, or have you always had some sense—well, let me put it this way: I have no doubt that you've always had a sense of the ideals your poems reach for, but when did you begin to feel that they were akin to s-f?*

WS   Actually, it would have surprised me to have anyone link most of my poems to s-f, back when I began to write; but once the surprise had worn off I think I would have felt sympathy for the ways of s-f, the ways of thinking, the freedom for excursions of thought.

And more recently, with the increase of science and its surprises in our daily lives—space travel, speed of transport, television, genetic experiments, and so forth—it's natural that these enhancements of imagination should be recognized and welcomed in the thought of all of us. My own natural daily impulses feel more related to these advances now; and my poems have more overt references to the wonders.

GVT   *A kind of direct stimulation of the imagination? Or do you find that your imagination seeks out the connections?*

WS   Well, writing always feels like roving around, accepting leads that occur as a result of the activity itself; and when the habits linked to science are a part of your life and your vocabulary, those links are not so much sought out as just welcomed.

GVT *That ties in with something you said earlier, about the ideas that come to you in writing poetry bouncing off "advances in speculation and knowledge that derive from science." It seems to be reciprocal in some of the science magazines*—Science '84, *for example, which is published by the American Association for the Advancement of Science, has been regularly publishing poetry since 1982, very solid science and speculative poems that are also aesthetically well done...* [Regrettably, it has since ceased publication, Ed.]

WS Yes, the kinship works both ways. Years ago a biochemist friend of mine published a poem in *The Scientific American*. He helped me to realize how the practice of being a scientist links to the speculative, conceptualizing activity of being a poet. Bronowski, early in his career of bringing science before the public, wrote a book about Blake. In one of his talks Oppenheimer said he had to choose between his commitment to poetry and his commitment to science.

The actual time a writer devotes to working with words mostly precludes two careers at once, but many people have noted the harmony between those impulses that lead into literature and those that lead into science. By the way, Bronowski's *Science and the Imagination* is a book that examines how the course of literature and the major developments in science paralleled each other from the time of the Renaissance.

GVT *That's interesting, about Bronowski writing a book on Blake, who was almost completely opposed to the "experimentalists," as he called scientists. He regarded Newton as being utterly satanic. Measuring and quantifying the world was, for him, an offense against the immeasurable majesty of God. I think he was unaware of the fact that Newton's* Principia *was his own poetic way of describing the beauty of God's cosmic handiwork; his lexicon was that of mathematical equations, and the scientific imagination that conceived the grand order of the heavens was inspired by religious fervor. Come to think of it, for all of his railing against science, Blake was doing pretty much the same thing—if you accept the idea that putting words to things, employing language to describe the world, is a kind of measuring and quantifying.*

WS   Blake's imagination interested Bronowski; that part is clear. But there was another aspect of Blake, too, that appealed—his social conscience. My abiding impression of Blake's most strong feelings is that he was appalled by industry and the form it was taking in England at the time. Not the spaciousness and imagination of science, but its apparent link to the "dark satanic mills" was Blake's beef.

GVT   *He may have been perceiving a connection between science and social consciousness that was not so obvious until the advent of the atomic bomb. Until physicists stood in their bunker at Alamagordo and cracked open the foundation of the universe, science had almost always been regarded as something removed from the concerns of the mundane world. But after the A-bomb, look what happened—suddenly the implications where quite clear as to how pure research can affect societies. With it came the efforts of scientists like Einstein, Oppenheimer, and Heisenberg, and writers like Bronowski, to "humanize" science by fostering a broad cultural awareness about the pursuit of knowledge of the physical universe. Some of the strongest appeals were made to art and imagination.*

WS   The tag I think of for this split is "The Two Cultures" tag, about a split that must be mended. Blake felt it, the danger, and I think of someone earlier, like John Donne. In our time, of course, the power of science has become terrifying, an emergency we are scrambling to overcome. We can't endure the split—it's too dangerous.

GVT   *How do you think s-f fits—if it does—into that "humanizing" of science?*

WS   Even when s-f makes science more scary and overwhelming, the directing of our attention is there. I think s-f is one of the inevitable human manifestations—a free and imaginative exploring of unmapped areas by that greatest of voyagers, the mind.

GVT   *I know it's hard to pin down definitions for viable art forms—precise definitions are, I think, a kind of autopsy—but what do you think the s-f ideal is?*

WS   As shadowed forth in some of the reactions preceding, I guess I would link s-f to freedom and range in thought, plus a readiness to accept extreme and bizarre ideas on a temporary basis for speculation and enjoyment. The appetite I sense in this area is that for spice, for the unusual, the unheard-of that possesses appeal once it *is* heard of.

GVT   *The "unusual, the unheard-of"—I like that. Some would also say "the bizarre" aspect creates a close kinship between s-f and the surreal. Has surrealism ever held much appeal for you, or do you feel that there's an important qualitative difference between the s-f and surreal orientations?*

WS   For a quick bid to engage on this topic I'll hazard that there is a profound difference. I think that the surreal is deliberately dazzling and confusing, or at least willing to be confusing, but that the best s-f can pursue actuality as closely as possible but be ready to range into what becomes—perforce—confusing.

The willed dazzle of surrealism has always thrown me off a bit; but the commitment to extrapolation in s-f has won me over.

GVT   *Samuel R. Delany, in a book of essays titled* The Jewel-Hinged Jaw, *made an interesting comparison between poetry and s-f. The essence of his comparison was that at root, poetry shares with s-f the attempt to describe* states of mind *rather than the external world. In this sense they're both aimed at the* ideal. *I'm wondering how that strikes you, or if the division between external and state-of-mind "reality" works for you in terms of your writing.*

WS   Speaking of "the ideal" makes me nervous; but it has often struck me that all of us—not just s-f people and other literary people, but all of us—find our way into contact with outside "reality" by means of states of mind. There is no other way, alas, but through the connections that our senses have to make; and our senses do not operate without the intervention of that "god within the mind" that governs the in-and-out activity of a conscious being.

Dealing directly with reality is impossible. Only through elaborations and complexities are we able to compare sense impressions, readings of instruments, findings of others, and thus converge—or apparently converge—with those parts of nature not available to our blunt senses.

GVT   *I don't know if I'd go so far as to say that formal scientific inquiry is basically a description of a state of mind—it's a philosophical labyrinth filled with trapdoors—though certainly the scientific method is a reflection of a state of mind, a conscious commitment to verify the nature of external reality through experiments that provide us with a range of facts. Now ordering those facts into a theoretical framework bears directly upon a state of mind. That's one of Bronowski's central points in* Science and the Imagination. *Once one has collected sufficient data, one must interpret it, and it strikes me that the interpretive act, rooted in and enabled by imagination, describes a state of mind. Kuhn, in* The Structure of Scientific Revolutions, *consistently avoids calling theory construction a description of "reality," preferring the term "model of" to indicate something that is always in a state of flux.*

This reminds me of something Joyce Carol Oates said a few years back—that writers (and I assume she included poets) do not actually attempt to depict the world as it "really is" but are merely advancing their own particular theories, their interpretations, of the world for verification or refutation by the reading public at large. I have always felt that speculation plays a strong role here. It's a two-sided matter, of course. On the one hand there's speculation that doesn't depart very far from verifiable facts, while on the other there's the speculative/imaginative—science fiction—which leaves the verifiable far behind.

WS   You hand me a couple of hot potatoes there, and I'll juggle them just a bit. I prefer that "model of" phrasing because I too am leery of pretending to link my ideas with something that is beyond me—"reality." That's one hot potato, just located, not dealt with.

The other one is about Joyce Carol Oates's phrasing: When I write, I suspect I am verging into new visions rather than identifying for others the visions I already have. I believe that the language itself helps form what I write. In other words, I want to emphasize the creative activity of writing (and talking) rather than the conceptualizing of being an author as being someone who uses language to transfer preexisting concepts to others. The language creates, when I write. I feel like a secretary available for whatever surfaces at the time.

GVT   *You mean that you often have no idea of what, precisely, you're going to write about until you write it?*

WS   The language intervenes—it influences what you say. But I do have an idea of what I'm going to write about—the process is not aimless. But once the process gets entangled with language it gets caught up in the cadences, the spooky mutual influence of syllables, the whole tapestry already present in the patterns of words. (Even in that sentence I just said I can perceive that my forward motion took advantage of sounds and images.)

GVT   *I'm thinking here of something Loren Eiseley wrote about language in his essay, "The Immense Journey," about the psychological evolution of humankind: "He was becoming something the world had never seen before—a dream animal—living at least partially within a secret universe of his own creation and sharing that secret universe in his head with other, similar heads. Symbolic communication had begun."*

WS   Think of the richness that comes into our consciousness! But sometimes I brood about what we may have lost when we diverged from the more direct, the animal, ways. Once in early light I was walking onto the University of Alaska campus in Fairbanks. I was looking for the Gruening Building—I was looking for the words. But something about that glorious light made me hark to this: If I didn't know how to read, maybe I would be seeing better, not just recognizing, but seeing.

GVT   *I'm getting a sense of where the speculative might fit in here, and by extension the imaginative. It lies in the act of interpreting what you know about the world around you. Of course, what you're interested in affects your range; you can stay tightly focused on the very particular—the so-called "realistic"—or you can cast-off all lines to chart new routes into the unknown, or move in any number of directions between the two extremes. Here again Bronowski seems to have addressed the issue in something he wrote in* A Sense of the Future: *"Poetry is as species-specific to man as science is, and though its forms lean more openly on metaphor than those of science, they are based equally on cognitive statement."*

WS   You make me think of something. Wouldn't it be good if s-f writers would combine their range of speculation with that kind of stubborn seeking-of-depth there in Bronowski and others like him who are trying to understand systematically? Someday there will be an author who writes so well that the writing will converge—not just by chance, but by its relentless cogency—with science itself.

GVT   *Not good—great! That's the ideal that works at the back of many s-f writers thoughts as they work at their craft—it's certainly at the back of mine, but I catch only glimpses of that great fusion. Olaf Stapledon, in* Last and First Men, The Star Mill *and* The Maker of Universes *attempted this fusion, but his language just was not up to the task—the fiction reads like very dry philosophy, cogent and inspiring in the scope and range of thought, but unconvincing as fiction, and in the end, too metaphysical. Thomas Mann was after the same thing in* The Magic Mountain, *and Herman Hesse in* The Glass Bead Game. *Perhaps poetry in our time will be the leading edge that draws the scientific/speculative into the full range of literature.*

WS   Let's hope that poetry can help, at least. Those continually new glimpses that science offers are certainly enticing. And just helping to keep that universe human is challenge enough for us all.

GVT   *There are those who sneer at the thought of science fiction, who would find the idea of "s-f poetry" to be ludicrous. You don't find the idea ludicrous, but what do you think it has to offer?*

WS   The way literature differs from life—the main way—for me, is in the direction of the new, unusual, beyond-the-borders kind of appeal. Thinking is fast experimenting, with light materials, such as fancy, imagination, the what-if impulse. You use up life and its plodding ways at a great rate, in literature; and I think s-f is one of the currently appealing channels for that kind of adventuring with the mind.

GVT   *Yes. Given that what you've said is the case, it seems such a shame that somebody would arbitrarily cut off the avenue for the new and experimental. But these entail taking chances. Do you think that's why some critics dismiss the s-f approach to poetry—or just writing in general— because of its departure from the safe ground of traditional approaches?*

WS   There must be many reasons for being arbitrary, and no doubt ignorance of the rich possibilities would rank pretty high. But if I take the put-down seriously and think about some good reasons for it, one does come to mind: perhaps many good people feel that slow, verifiable, cumulative approaches to understanding are essential. Such people might be made nervous by s-f—and perhaps made nervous by poetry as such, or by fiction as such. Or maybe such people could abide realistic fiction but not the kind that flies through the night and darkness. I don't know.

GVT   *The idea that a particular approach to literature is inherently frivolous, though, just doesn't work. All approaches can be frivolous or serious. It depends on the skill, the talent, and the interest of the artist to make it one or the other.*

WS   Part of what you said makes me think of this: Just as an author might converge toward the science part of s-f, so a scientist might converge toward the fiction part. Science today seems to require such quick adjustments in speculation, so many alternatives for explaining phenomena, that it seems like the rapid considering of helpful fictions.

GVT   *Have you ever sensed a general reluctance on the part of many poets to deal with science? There was a time, I believe, when some of them found it fashionable to put down Science as inherently alien to the poetic impulse.*

WS   There is a general impression that a choice has to be made—be hard headed and scientific or be vague but warm and human and poetic. And most poets I know shy away from science and its values. In practice, this alienation may not do much damage, for we are all forced to live in the presence of both ranges of values, but there is a weakening of joint endeavors and a loss of mutual enrichment. Over the years many coercive examples demonstrate the power of being open to science— the story of Milton visiting Galileo, Pope incorporating the ideas of his time into his poetry, Goethe being hungry for understanding the processes of biology. And there are scientists whose writings demonstrate how the language performs for those who carry into it the habits of scientific thought—Pascal, Descartes, Whitehead.

GVT   *That's so right! And I think I'd add to them Poincaré, Bertrand Russell, Loren Eiseley. Scientists, philosophers, mathematicians all. Some were even poets—Goethe for one, Eiseley for another;—and lest I forget, America's first technological poet, Walt Whitman. He wasn't afraid of the new, of the scientific or technological. He was a real renaissance poet.*

WS   Even a whiff of that list of yours makes me want to extend it, and to join such company!

Stafford
Van Troyer

GVT *We haven't said anything yet about craft. Have you read much specifically science and s-f related poetry? What do you generally think of the craftsmanship exhibited by a lot of it?*

WS Despite the theoretical linkage between the attitudes that enable science and those that enable poetry, I have found very little poetry that measures up to that assumed potential.

Maybe those prevalent attitudes mentioned earlier have diverted the best talents from any sustained literary use of science. Maybe there's something in literary tastes of our time that induces only superficial uses of current discovery

Maybe some barrier prevents anyone from carrying the tentativeness and specifics of science into the language experience that enables poetry. A poem has to fly. It must not be encumbered by some of those warnings and strictures and hesitations that accompany advances in knowledge of the unknown aspects of things. But it might be that s-f, with its willing suspension of verification, could be an avenue for writers to help us all participate in the exhilaration of discovery. We can expand our experience and still not encumber the orderly, workaday part of science that is needed for incremental advance into the unknown-that-works.

GVT *There is a certain barrier, though I don't think it's necessarily one of artistic limitations (except as arbitrarily imposed) so much as one of knowledge. Like all art, poetry partakes of shared cultural knowledge, which enables it to connect with, to address directly the emotions and avoid those encumbrances you mentioned. Perhaps it's just that, until recently, there wasn't enough generally shared knowledge about the joy, the spaciousness of scientific discovery, and how profoundly it affects all aspects of our lives. The recent popularity of science fiction in the movies and on television, as well as sophisticated science programs like Carl Sagan's PBS Cosmos series, have probably done quite a lot to enhance a general receptivity towards a greater fusion of scientific concepts in the arts.*

WS   That barrier you mentioned—that lack of enough generally shared knowledge—still operates, I'm afraid. We feel the need to get through that barrier, but the gulf between most of us and the requisite understanding may be getting wider. S-f lives in that area of human experience; we venture into it—and with added zest of late—but we may be more confused than ever.

GVT   *I read somewhere, once—I think it was in an* Oregonian *article—that you believed that anyone could write poetry, but that you had no doubt that you'd never be out of a job as a poet because too many people were convinced they couldn't do it. Care to elaborate on that?*

WS   That remark of mine is premised on the tendency of most people to assume that being bright and having ambition can suffice to bring about worthy literary works. It takes more than those qualities—it takes involvement in the processes of writing. It takes sustained relation to language in its state of being molten. It takes willingness to fail and try again. Most people who mention their admiration for poetry resemble people who say they would give anything if they could play the piano. They won't give what it takes. People are like that. So adepts in certain activities will always be a minority.

GVT   *When you begin a poem, are you first concerned with assigning it a particular form, or is the form something that grows out of the content of the poem as it evolves?*

WS   The form grows as the poem goes along. The form is part of the discovery process: the texture of the language begins to tell you what to do with it.

GVT   *Do you think poets ought to pay close attention to form? I'm thinking here about traditional as well as not-so-traditional forms.*

WS   Writers I know have knowledge that came to them as a result of their interests. They do know a lot about forms and such, but not as a duty. If you study forms in order to be a writer, you probably don't have the gusto that brings about real, interiorized relation to language. Dutiful artists have started from the wrong place . . . . It may be that anyone with an appetite for doing art will be protected against being trapped by mechanics, for that appetite will lead to experiments and excitements, no matter how much control someone else tries to impose.

GVT   *[Robert Frazier], editor of the anthology of s-f poetry* Burning With a Vision, *wrote in his introduction that "since scientific concepts are the most powerful in our times... poets can use them to good advantage. The two large schools of modern poetry, Deep Imagist and Confessional, appear weakened by repetition and a lack of emotive power. They fossilize, clinging tenaciously to the past... Poetry can only benefit from a blood transfusion from the future..." That's a pretty strong statement. What do you think about it? How do you feel about schools of thought (or aesthetic concerns) as they apply to poetry?*

WS   Preaching to poets about what they should have a conscientious interest in is like guiding scientists toward worthy engineering enterprises. It seems efficient but it may violate an essential in the process of being relied on. No doubt many schools of writing do weaken through repetition and lack of emotive power, but such is the lot of human beings; we can't always be succeeding. We must, however, if we are in science or the arts, find our lonely ways by what interests us, not by what governments or critics perceive as a good way for us to go.

Schools of thought may appeal to individual artists; s-f has its own flavor and enticement, and individual artists deserve reminders about available experiences for them. But after the reminders, after the realizations, the artist goes on by means of appetite, by means of emerging discoveries within the practice of the art. S-f lives by its new turns, its unpredictability; and so does poetry. The two have many opportunities, and some of them may converge. But not through deliberate planning.

Art is different from that. Like other activities that flourish because of sustained, frequent involvement, writing succeeds through the individual's commitment to it, through the artist's familiarity with the materials and processes of writing. But that involvement has to combine the "hard work" part with an appetite, a zest. Your heart has to be in it. The effort alone won't do it; and the fervent desire—the heart—won't do it alone. but combined, action and commitment can result in quality performance.

GVT   *To listen to some poets, one would get the impression that* form *is the central concern of the poem. I get the feeling that in their canon, art is the result of deliberate planning, and if it lacks an identifiable form it is something less than art.*

WS   There's a hidden element in the issue as posed. The finished work will have a pattern, a trajectory; it will succeed because of the resonances within the material and aptness between that material and its way of application. Hence the assessment that the artist must have planned those resonances. But to the artist in words, the language may just feel good in certain moves and not others; the apparent pattern comes not from trying to fit a pattern envisioned beforehand, but from yielding to the signals received in the doing of the poem.

And the finished poem will have felicities for which the critics haven't yet found terms of identification, except in broad categories of little use to the practicing writer...

Maybe we should relax about *a priori* decisions about the worth of a what we do. If we find our way to satisfying activities that result in something that satisfies others like ourselves, then we are certainly accomplishing some kind of human achievement. I don't believe I want to assure myself of critic's approval before working out my kind of writing. If I stray into disapproved ways, I can suffer the disapproval, and probably regret it. But I can't guide myself by any assessments that paralyze my way of proceeding...

Just as being too much controlled by immediate engineering needs could inhibit a scientist, or being held to immediate test results could dull the life of a teacher. We need freedom to fail, to try out our wilder ideas. Otherwise we may miss the momentum needed for bigger accomplishments.

GVT   *You have consistently spoken of speculation, the unknown-that-works, the imagination. Your dedication to imagination seems almost Blakeian.*

WS   That label feels so good that I won't quarrel with it, though it might have implications that would trouble me if I were smart enough to perceive them. I'll embrace your term and be ready to appease the spirit of Blake some time, if I meet it . . .

GVT   *Imagination can take you down some wild roads, and you need talent and a willingness to travel them, to depart from the acceptable, and describe the sights along the way. That earned Blake the reputation for being something of a crank, and his poetry was not taken very seriously during his lifetime.*

WS   His production strains our ability to follow, and sometimes that strain is too much for me. But where I can keep up, his poems are marvelous.

GVT   *Blake occupies a prominent place in your vocation as a writer, doesn't he? Is this because of his social consciousness or the breadth of this vision?*

WS   In the course of his cranky dreaming he touched upon issues that occupy artists; so it just happens that some of his phrasings have become a part of my mental furniture. His sayings are so apt sometimes that I find myself relying on them. It's just the neatness of his language, I'm afraid, that has captured me

GVT   *In a recent letter you mentioned that you were working on a book on the writer's vocation, and said, "I am now envisioning having chapters that link to poetry and religion (!)..." That exclamation point after religion intrigues me. How is that surprising?*

WS   I find it natural to link religion and art. But my excuses are two. For one thing it was like a joke, to push you into the company of those who would be surprised. And then it is true that the topic is not prevalent among most poets today. But I think it very much worth pursuing, and I do intend to make it part of my book.

GVT   *For a long time I've considered the impulse behind art and science to be essentially a religious one. By that I don't mean the religious as usually associated with churches or received dogma, but the spiritual quest to give order to the universe, to establish cosmos, perspective, a sense of place in the order of things.*

WS   At home in our heads we are surrounded by mysteries that call us out and entice and surprise us. Some of our excursions are beliefs and theories, or science and religion, or s-f, or poetry... I want to take part in it all.

All the powers of the universe are potentially contained in man and his physical body, and all his organs are nothing but the products and representatives of the powers of nature.

Paracelsus

The model of the artist which is preserved in our cultural baggage is a model of a man (often) alone (yet more often). To break the first assumption has been a project of recent lifetimes of women. Breaking the second is a special project of *POLY.* The surrealists were among the first this century to value collaboration in poetry. Andre Breton coined the term Communicating Vessels (*Les Vases communicants*) to describe, among other things, the connecting structure of *action* and *the dream.* The term also suggests the conjunction of alchemical flasks, retorts and other vessels.

POLY adopts it in celebration of collaboration. First, Tom Disch and David Lehman's "Six Times Six, Plus Three, Times Four, in Five Seventy-Nine," was written after a meeting between them in 1979. Each wrote a sestina, using the same six end-words, making sure to choose one term of strange abstraction: *epithesis,* one of romantic longing: *elsewhere,* and a quartet of familiar nouns: *face, poker, violets, windows.* The results were then twice fused collaboratively into new sestinas.

David Lehman, writer and book critic for *Newsweek,* lives in Lansing, New York. His poems may be read in his forthcoming book from Princeton University Press, *An Alternative to Speech,* and in back issues of *Poetry, The Paris Review,* and *Partisan Review.*

Next, a collaboration between Kathryn Rantala and Lee Ballentine gives some of the flavor of *POLY*'s genesis. Rantala has published in *Burning With a Vision,* and in *Velocities, Portland Review, South Dakota Review,* and *Umbral.* Her two chapbooks *The Dark Man* and *The Brickbuilder* were published under the name K.E. Roney.

Rantala   It's the expansion of historical frames of reference besides expansion into space or the future that makes speculative/s-f poetry possible. If people writing in such a fluid, enlarged perspective can keep the language taut and non-proselike, a wider literary audience will recognize it.

More explication of the *POLY* concept follows. "The Fate of Polyphemus" is by Andrew Joron and Lee Ballentine, engaging in a form established by their earlier collaboration "Cascade" which was published in *Velocities*. Both have other poems in *POLY*.

At this point, *Communicating Vessels* moves into its logical extension. If as has been said, poetry is that which is lost in translation, then poetry "translation" can succeed only as collaboration between a poet and a poet-interpreter. A spectrum of contemporary and historical texts shows the international character of speculative poetry, and points toward its literary underpinnings.

John Oliver Simon begins, joining in the political and speculative preoccupations of contemporary poets Horacio Salas (Argentina), Oscar Hahn (Chile), and Alberto Blanco. "Mal de Ojo" appeared in *Voces y Fragmentos: Poesia Argentina de Hoy*, ed. Jorge Boccamera, Michoacan, Mexico, 1981. "Vision de Hiroshima" first appeared in *Arte de Morir*, Ruray, Lima, Peru, 1981. Their translations are original to *POLY*. "Un Transparente Dominio" and its translation are reprinted from *The Magazine of Speculative Poetry*. All are reprinted with permission.

Simon   My work over the last four years to learn Spanish and translate younger Latin American poets, and having my own work translated and published in Mexico, and now perhaps Nicaragua and Brazil, has added another world to my imagination, another hemisphere to my brain. And an awareness that the metaphorical realities of poetry imply life-and-death commitments in the political imaginary outer-space world we happen to be living on in this grim poetic fiction here.

Michael Hamburger has translated the work of Gunter Grass, Hugo von Hofmannsthal, Holderlin, Brecht, Rilke, and Georg Trakl, among others. In *Communicating Vessels*, he explores roots of speculative poetry in the fantastic, rendering "Decline" and "Lament" by Trakl. These sombre short poems have seldom appeared in the United States, here reprinted by permission of Logbridge-Rhodes Inc. Hamburger appears also among the *POLY Singularities*.

Born in Salzburg in 1886, Trakl was trained as a dispensing chemist. After performances of two of his plays and a year of military service, he planned emigration to Borneo. In 1912, success with *Der Brenner* in Innsbruck intervened; his two books-of-poems were published in the following two years. After being posted to Galicia as a lieutenant in the medical corps, Trakl was in August, 1914 charged with the care of 90 hopeless casualties. He broke-down and was imprisoned at Crakow under observation for schizophrenia, where he died in November, 1914 of an overdose of cocaine.

Yves Troendle next interprets five poems by Tristan Tzara and one by Hans Arp.

Troendle   Poetry is how language can explore itself. It has long been the antidote to the incrustations of political propaganda and psychological cliches. Perhaps its most vital foci today were pointed out by Freud (leading to surrealism), and more recently, the Post-Structuralists (leading to poetries that explore the tissue of language as constitutive of social being and the reflective self).

Troendle, whose work also appears in the *POLY Singularities*, here focuses his attention on founding practitioner and proponent of sur-realism Tristan Tzara. Dada was proclaimed in 1916 Zurich by Huelsenbeck, Hugo Ball, Arp, et al., and Tzara, who wrote of himself perhaps, in *The Antihead:* "I also have had wings for caressing in a lim-pid language which barely touched me."

Of Hans Arp (who also used the name *Jean*) it is said that on being called for military service, he reported to the German Consulate in Zurich, and on entering the examination room, crossed himself in front of a portrait of Marshal Hindenburg. When asked for his age, he wrote his birthdate *16 September 1887* a number of times, drew a line underneath, and produced a gigantic sum. He was excused. More certainly, Arp is one of a very few ever genuinely to excel as poet *and* plastic artist.

Finally a sample of the *homolinguistic translation* of Douglas Barbour, who here takes Yeats as a starting point for an experiment in meaning.

Barbour   Where translation is perceived as a transfer of language from one code to another, *homolinguistic translation* is a transfer from one code to another *within the same language.* As in all translation, there is an original text, a system of transfer, and a new text. In all such transla-tion, a sense of play is paramount, yet not without serious intent. "Words, Perhaps, for Music" is an example of *structural translation*, which uses the words of the original text in some manner, here by choos-ing one *per line in the order the lines appear in the original, and seek-ing to create meaningful if minimal texts from those given words.*

Disch

Lehman

SIX TIMES SIX, PLUS THREE,
TIMES FOUR, IN FIVE SEVENTY-NINE

FLYING HOME

At the moment of lift-off out of the window
The patterned world becomes its own epithesis,
Unwitnessed by the passengers. To prefer poker
To the tragic sense of space, to turn one's face
From the blank heaven here to homilies of violets
Is a vice as human as failure. Elsewhere

We might feel less overawed—not in that elsewhere
Sprawling in off-white washes beyond the windows'
Double-glass, but in some reasonable glade of violets
And primroses, in ordinary houses, where an epithesis
Of unbearable stresses may be encountered face to face,
Eyeball to eyeball, as at the supreme moment of poker,

The moment of surmise. What kinship there is in poker,
What comfort, what values palpably shared. Elsewhere
Than over its green baize could any of us face
The prospect of returning to the world these windows
Still so graciously seal from us? Could we defer epithesis,
Or even define it? As well attempt to pilfer violets

From the wallpaper. Do you remember that design? The violets
So stylized and bright, a grid of purple poker
Chips imposed on the roses' silly, sweet epithesis,
A Vasarely out of Grandma Moses, a paper elsewhere
Punctuated by a fireplace and curtained windows;—
So safe: as though one's favorite familiar face

Had blossomed endlessly out of it, floral face
Succeeding face, profuse as actual violets;
Safe as the domestic minute when the windows
Incandesce to mirrors, when tongs and poker
Reassure us we shall arrive no elsewhere
Than exactly here, in this serene epithesis;—

Though yet we're only halfway home, and air's epithesis
Is all uncertainty, a veil of vapor drawn across the face
Of what we must believe is real. Someone, elsewhere,
May arrange a welcoming vase of violets,
But I am here, forever, eavesdropping on a game of poker,
Filling the emptiness of fictive windows

With windows from which the unthinkable epithesis
Of the smile implicit in your theoretic poker-face
Sprinkles a spring of violets on this world of elsewhere.

Tom Disch

Disch

Lehman

Not to discover, but to station themselves behind shuttered windows,
Away from the nearest friendly epithesis,
Eyeball to eyeball, as at the supreme moment of poker,
Like a howl of uncertainty, a veil of vapor drawn across the face
From some unnamed place off-stage, they come bearing no bouquets of
    violets;
And when they pack their knapsacks, heading for elsewhere,

They instantly discard them upon arrival. But we (who shall arrive no
    elsewhere
Safe as the domestic minute of windows
That arrange a welcoming vase of violets)
Expect no applause, except from within. The epithesis
Of bearable stresses may be encountered in this face
Of October: cold, serene, and as indifferent as Cezanne's poker—

Playing, pipe-smoking peasants, to us. At the supreme moment of poker
None of this matters. Off we go, on another anxious journey elsewhere
To the tragic sense of space, to turn a factual face
From the emptiness of fictive windows
As though to a wedding, as though seeking an epithesis
Double-glass, but in some reasonable glade of violets

Since death alone is eternal, and comes armed with violets.
But I am here, forever, eavesdropping on a game of poker.
The brass and winds come first; they announce a new epithesis
Of what we must believe is real. A messenger from elsewhere
Confirms the prognosis, the darkness coming up to the windows
And blossoming endlessly out of them, floral face

Succeeding face, but the strings lag behind; on the conductor's face
Of disaster is a noble chin. He withdraws his gift of violets
And returns us to the world of beckoning windows
Unwitnessed by the passengers. Then he scatters a bag of poker
Chips and issues instructions as to their use, here and elsewhere,
Among primroses, in ordinary houses, where an epithesis

Of fear awaits us. The verdict is an unthinkable epithesis
But a cheerful one withal, a laying on of gloved hands, in the face
Of values palpably shared, like a bottle of wine. Elsewhere
From this blank heaven, away from homilies to dying violets, *Disch*
Our friends the reformed rapists are playing nickel and dime poker *Lehman*
In a living room punctuated by a fireplace and curtained windows.

They defer the definition of epithesis, with thanks for the worthless violets.
As though aping the full moon, you maintain your poker face
Throughout, and point to the windows, and dream of elsewhere.

Tom Disch & David Lehman

Disch

Lehman

"The darkness comes up to the windows,
But there's no honey in it; it's April but it feels like an epithesis
Of October, cold, serene, as indifferent as Cezanne's poker
Playing, pipe-smoking peasants, to us. A smile has frozen on my face
But not by chance. Many thanks for your gift of violets
Although they're worthless, and other reminders of an opulent elsewhere."

Off they go, on another anxious journey elsewhere,
Not to discover, but to station themselves behind shuttered windows,
Since death alone is eternal. They come armed with violets
As though to a wedding, as though seeking an epithesis
Of cheer, a laying on of gloved hands, in the face
Of certain failure, and luckless nights of beer and poker.

A frozen leg of lamb will serves as well as a red-hot poker
For a murder weapon, contrary to what I have elsewhere
Reported, provided you have nerve enough to face
The music and resist the temptation of beckoning windows.
Expect no applause, except from within. The epithesis
Of disaster is a noble chin, an early grave, with violets.

"The answer is known, but not to you: a repudiation of violets.
The answer is silence, like the fear of calling a bluff in poker
Because maybe it is no bluff at all, but an epithesis
Once known, now no longer: the answer, in short, is elsewhere
Not now, not yet: the eyes blur, looking at simultaneous windows,
Looking in the mirror, and seeing an unfamiliar juvenile face."

There was a time when divine good looks, a classical face,
Assured one of success: hundreds to attend the funeral: violets
Galore: now, however, the best we can do is pot our impatiens on
   windows—
Ills: reformed rapists play nickel-and-dime poker
In our living rooms: to the lighthouse we must not go, but elsewhere
Away from the sphere of our sorrow, to the nearest friendly epithesis.

The brass and winds come first: they announce a new epithesis
Like a howl, but the strings lag behind; on the conductor's face
A growing anxiety can be seen, as the messenger enters from elsewhere,
From some unnamed place off-stage, bearing a bouquet of violets
to disguise his bad news. "Mr Wright, who sent these, cannot play poker
With you, later tonight; he is in Washington, smashing windows."

Disch
Lehman

The darkness comes up to the windows, in an epithesis
Of fear: we face the god we fear: we fear violets
And must go elsewhere: the poker game is over.

David Lehman

Disch

Lehman

At the moment the darkness comes up to the windows
The patterned world becomes its own epithesis
Of October, cold, serene, and as indifferent as Cezanne's poker
Playing, pipe-smoking peasants. To turn one's face
From the blank heaven here to your gift of violets
Is a vice as human as failure would be elsewhere.

Off they go, on another anxious journey elsewhere,
To discover off-white washes behind the shuttered windows'
Double-glass. Death alone comes armed with violets
And primroses, as though to a wedding where an epithesis
Of bearable stresses may be encountered in the face
Of certain failure, as at the supreme moment of poker.

A moment of surmise will serve as well as a red-hot poker
For a murder weapon: values palpably shared. Elsewhere
Than over this green baize could any of us face
The music or resist the temptation of beckoning windows?
Expect no applause, except from within. The epithesis
Of disaster is a noble chin. As well attempt to pilfer violets

From the wallpaper. Remember your repudiation of violets
So stylized and bright, a grid of purple poker
Chips imposed on the roses' bluff: a sweet epithesis
Once known, now no longer, the answer to a paper elsewhere.
Not now, not yet: the eyes blur, looking at curtained windows,
Looking in the mirror and seeing one's favorite familiar face.

There was a time when divine good looks, classical face
Succeeding face, profuse as actual violets,
Assured one of success: now we can only let the windows
Incandesce to mirrors. Rapists playing nickel-and-dime poker
Reassure us we shall arrive no elsewhere
Than exactly here, our sphere of sorrow in this serene epithesis.

The brass and winds come first, announcing the air's epithesis
Like a howl of uncertainty, a veil of vapor drawn across the face
Of what we must believe, as the messenger enters from elsewhere,
Disguising his bad news with a welcoming vase of violets: *Disch*
"I am here, but Mr. Wright, who sent these, cannot play poker *Lehman*
Tonight; he is in Washington, filling fictive windows

With darkness." Windows from which the unthinkable epithesis
Of the face implicit in your theoretic fear of violets
sprinkles an elsewhere of poker chips on a world that's all over.

Tom Disch & David Lehman

The following dialogue was conducted in the summer of 1985. The eponym *The Incense Salesman* is worth glossing—it was used for many years by Oregon poet Michael Marsh, to whom for his conversation and inspiration, many thanks.

POLY I'm writing to invite your participation in a literary experiment, a kind of yearbook of speculative poetry to appear next year. I hope you will contribute, perhaps a poem which might not appear elsewhere because of its length, or its danger to prudery or to narrowness of imagination.

Rantala Thanks for your invitation. I am in one of those warps of frantic nonproductivity—a chronosynclasticinfindibulum? Nothing so romantic, I'm sure. If I can manage to put heart and mind together (the result should be OK after "cooking" for so long), I'll certainly send it.

POLY You know, this project borrowed its name from a poem I wrote years ago. You might find in it some stimulus to your own writing for *POLY*.

Rantala
Ballentine

Father light stands naked on the roof
with a watering hose. A black lantern of wine.
With his throat swollen. For love of him
stiff women glad themselves in foils of talk
and rub white arms with keys from the hotel.
For the love of him — armies expend themselves
in sine-waves under a wheat sky
and aircraft genuflect.

Where the wet fell — POLYTRYWEG his daughter
orange her catchword — sent a ladder
of her sparrows into the gardens
where a boy hung smiling to dissuade him.

You are old — father.
Your missiles are slow as icebergs
while my orchards bloom.
My screen farms are rastered in color.
Come down among the suns!

But in his sad garden — strait and brown
are two empty buckets — and three towns.
A big knot is hidden somewhere.
Two ampoules of the world remain.
Orange his watchword.

Lee Ballentine

The doubles ooze,   *Rantala*
melt in their sex like cells: *Ballentine*
drool, albumen,
then two of them.
Short term,
shorter work.

They don't last,
in life either.
A neon,
a resort.
Doubling and doubling.
Who cares,
except for the drinks.

Somebody shot one,
or two.
they oozed,
both of them.
One had a gun.
A Saturday night special.

Kathryn Rantala

POLY   More material!

Rantala
Ballentine

This rose wafted here
a graft from under the door,
a spiral
from the Incense Salesman.

Last week brought the Ring People,
day after day
orbiting, searing a path
through weeds;
and, later, The Cord,
pulsing and uncoiling
his dark wrists.

And now, the predatory rose.

The censer sends them in:
a tangle of caves
and galleries,
damp wax,
curries, fur,
a hot conspiratorial sweat
and burned virgins.
Effluvia on all fours,
now pinned in the skin.

The Incense Salesman comes in,
a scent adrift.
A rose tattoo
and everything else
comes with him.

Kathryn Rantala

When a bee from one hive enters another, and
attempts to dance for his hosts, his information is not
intelligible to them. Their guest's dance, which was intended
to lead them to a bowl of sugar water, leads only to a
concrete Magdalene. What dances do the clones perform in
their house?

The skin, with no high albedo glancing laser shots, absorbs
color, is sold sometimes, reflective ensigns needled in a
cheap art-shop under the cityway. Rose. Tattoo. Where the
practice flourishes, some kinship obtains between an old
sailor with his ship named, girl with an orchid on her
breast, young men disfiguring each other in blue lines.

If scents are traded for living art, what other commodities
are quoted on the same exchange? A psychopomp?

Lee Ballentine

Rantala
Ballentine

A hawk
random branched ·
scans.
A lady,
an historical pomp,
a likely;
and she, the Apportionate,
steps in.

Then wings.
The sheer, slice,
bright red-browns,
the shrill edges,
wounds.
Contusus, Laceratus,
all the rotten little postcards.
Sufficient to shudder.
Spots, and blue,
too many spots.

Now touchless.
Flight,
bland flight.
Blank.
If he's careful.
If he's if he's careful.

Kathryn Rantala

The stars are down   *Rantala*
are coming   *Ballentine*
down.
Silken brothers,
woven,
spiral hairs streaming
down
celestial spears
streaming,
down.

Trying to,
finding,
trying
this way,
out
the impact,
implant,
exit all around.
A line of it.
An exit
wound.

Lachrima, lachrima,
Jesu falling
a star sword,
the skull, pierced,
deep, centered,
a freemason's
jewel
embedded,
emblazoned.
Supra
nova

                                        Kathryn Rantala

ANDREW JORON AND LEE BALLENTINE

THE FATE OF POLYPHEMUS

Joron

Ballentine   I.

Once infected, the seminal fact
Shakes like dewdrop, or an aerodrome
—unsealed, its one ray
May send words in round crescendo
Winter-white / showering into the microbial bath

So motionless a drama!—frescoes caught
In hues unknown to daylight
Torn from an antique Cinema of Plenty

Gauge of the lost: it is a probe landed inside our heads
An inhuman presence disguised as language
. . . test-chambers
Discharge the favorite tunes of the terminal comedian
A sky redolent with murals of rain
This plan of memory
Confined to the stochastic cage
        The armada of roseate skulls
        The extinction of far-away lights

                             II.

I— am water that concentrates the sun in the mouth of a
        blowfish two vivisectionists are dissecting
&—as they miscalculate atoms of the cave wall into
        color with their instruments
I become beast-soul in the cave

One of those hierarchies of crows that wind a cometary
        path where spires of a dead world sing to their
        ATHENA

My eye turns slow-logic to the next target — children
    wild around the lake — picking stems of violets
    preserved in the metal.
And as molecules of the air themselves grow faces
    of the grey-eyed goddess
    a ray of blood-light & information
Blew down the world's throat & exploded him.
The surface of the redact star
The fountain of the white crows

Joron
Ballentine

Horacio
Salas

Tal vez ese jaguar oscuro que cruza en la estación de Bulnes
y continúa distraídamente riendo con su amiga
el odio de esa muchacha que levantaba el whisky hasta los párpados
y dejó un gran ramo de rosas y también su tristeza
la huella o digamos la estela de sus pasos o del Bountry
antes de divisar las islas
sabiendo que eran perseguidos por galeones reales
la timidez detrás de los anteojos oscuros
aquel espejo enmarcado de árboles que ya no habrá de verte
o las fotografías en pose de los abuelos
mirando. El lago de lost cisnes desde un palco
clavados en la nuca como si fueran dos balas asesinas
en elcuerpo de un hombre torturado
puñales a milímetros de ese rostro perfecto
el balazo que apaga un cigarillo
o inundados de lágrimas al descubrir
que el amor también podía ser triste
temblorosa como el hilo de una tela de araña que cuelga desde el techio
(y la noche del río era una guitarra pulsada por un ciego
o encontrarte de pronto en una calle
con la mirada de lost gatos siameses entre los brazos de las hechiceras
y aun desde un afiche con un dedo meñique entre los dientes
lo cierto es que de todas formas el virus se introduce en el cuerpo
se aloja en los pulmones te muerde entre las vértebras
destroza los omóplatos resbala hasta el estómago
Sólo una cuerda roja en la muñeca izquierda
puede servir de antídoto contra lost meleficios
Sin embargo
nunca habre de entender que tanto amor
se arroje
así
por la ventana

Horacio

Salas

Maybe that dark jaguar cruising Bulnes station
who goes laughing spaced out with his girl friend,
the hate of that girl who raised her whiskey to her eyelids
leaving behind a big bouquet of roses as well as her sadness,
the track or let's say the wake of her steps
or of the *Bounty*
before dispersing themselves among the islands
knowing they were pursued by royal frigates,
timidity behind dark glasses
that mirror framed with trees which won't have seen you yet
or photographs in a pose of grandparents
looking. The lake with swans below the box seats
nailed in the neck as if by two assassin's bullets
in the body of a tortured man
daggers millimeters from that perfect face
the shot that puts out a cigarette,
or inundated with tears to discover
that love can also be sad
shaking like the thread of a spiderweb hanging from the roof
(and the river's night was a guitar strummed by a blind man)
or to meet you suddenly in a cafe
with the regard of siamese cats in the arms of a sorceress
or even under a poster with a little finger between the teeth,
we only know that somehow the virus enters the body
lodges in the lungs, bites you between the ribs
destroys the red blood cells, slides toward the abdomen.
Only a red cord around the left wrist
will serve as an antidote against these evils.
Nevertheless
I will never have to understand how so much love
could throw itself
like this
out the window.

translated by John Oliver Simon

Oscar

Hahn

arrojó sobre la triple ciudad un proyectil único,
cargado con la potencia del universo.

Mamsala Purva
Texto sánscrito milenario

Ojo con el ojo numeroso de la bomba,
que se desata bajo hongo vivo.
Con el fulgor del Hombre no vidente, ojo y ojo.

Los ancianos huían decapitados por el fuego,
encallaban los ángeles en cuernos sulfúricos
decapitados por el fuego,
se varaban las vírgenes de aureola radiactiva
decapitadas por el fuego
Todos los niños emigraban decapitados por el cielo.
No el ojo manco, no la piel tullida, no sangre
sobre la calle derretida vimos:
los amantes sorprenididos en la cópula,
petrificados por el magnésium del infierno,
los amantes inmóviles en la vía pública,
y la mujer de Lot
convertida en columna de uranio.
El hospital caliente se va por los desagües,
se va por las letrinas tu corazón helado,
se van a gatas por debajo de las camas,
se van a gatas verdes e incendiadas
que maúllan cenizas.
La vibración de las aguas hace blanquear al cuervo
y ya no puedes olvidar esa piel adherida a los muros
porque derrumbamiento beberás, leche en escombros.
Vimos las cúpulas fosforecer, los ríos
anaranjados pastar, los puentes preñados
parir en medio del silencio.
El color estridente desgarraba
el corazón de sus propios objetos:
el rojo sangre, el rosado leucemia,
el lacre llaga, enloquecidos por la fisión.

he hurled upon the triple city a single
projectile, charged with the energy of the universe.

Oscar

Hahn

Mamsala Purva
Sanskrit text a thousand years old

Eye to the numerous eye of the bomb
as it unleashes under the living mushroom.
With the splendor of the unforeseeing Human, eye and eye.

Old men fled decapitated by fire,
the angels founder in horns of sulfur
decapitated by fire,
the virgins with radioactive halos ran aground
decapitated by fire.
All the children ran away decapitated by the sky.
On the molten street we saw
no maimed eye, no slashed skin, no blood:
lovers surprised in copulation,
petrified by magnesium of inferno,
lovers immobile in the public street,
and Lot's wife
turned into a column of uranium.
The scorching hospital runs down the drain
your frozen heart goes down the toilet,
they run on all fours under the bed,
they go on all fours green and burning
howling out ash.
Vibration of waters turns the crow white
and you can't forget the skin stuck to the wall
for you will drink demolition, milk of rubble.
We saw the towers glowing,
the yellowed rivers grazing,
the bridges give birth in silence.
Strident color ripped the heart
away from its own objects:
red blood, pink leukemia,
scarlet wound, maddened by fission.

Oscar
Hahn

El aceite nos arrancaba los dedos de los pies,
las sillas golpeaban las ventanas
flotando en marejadas do ojos,
los edificios licuados se veían chorrear
por troncos de árboles sin cabeza,
y entre las vias lácteas y las cáscaras,
soles o cerdos luminosos
chapotear en las charcas celestes.

Por los peldaños radiactivos suben los pasos,
suben los peces quebrados por el aire fúnebre.
¿Y qué haremos con tanta ceniza?

Oil tore off the toes of our feet,
chairs slammed the windows
floating in waves of eyes,
the liquid buildings dripped
by headless trunks of trees,
and between the milky ways and waterfalls
luminous pigs or suns
splashed in celestial pools.

Footsteps climb the radioactive stairs,
broken fish rise through the grieving air,
And what will we do with so much ash?

Oscar
Hahn

translated by John Oliver Simon

a M.C. Escher

Alberto
Blanco

El punto no tiene dirección.
El punto no tiene sentido.
El principio de todas las cosas
no es más que la intersección
do los líneas que se atraen:
En el punto se define una estrategia.

La línea es el punto en movimiento
hacia el universo de la dimensión.
La l'ínea tiene sentido y se dirige.
No es más que la intersección
de dos superficies que viajan:
Se puede recorrer todo su largo.

La superficie es la línea en movimiento
hacia la caravana de las dimensiones.
La superficie es extensa y plana.
No es más que la intersección
de dos volúmenes que se encuentran:
Se puede escribir y dibujar sobre ella.

El volumen es la superficie en movimiento
fuera de sí por la noche que vemos.
De día es la resistencia de la sombra.
El volumen no es más que la intersección
de dos tiempos completos en un cuerpo:
Aquí se lucha y se sabe, se ama y se calla.

to M.C. Escher

The point has no direction.   *Alberto*
The point has no meaning.   *Blanco*
The beginning of everything
is no more than the intersection
of two lines which attract each other:
The point defines a strategy.

The line is the point in motion
toward the dimensional universe.
The line has meaning and makes its way.
It is not more than the intersection
of two travelling surfaces:
You can run through its whole length.

The surface is the line in motion
toward the caravan of dimensions.
The surface is broad and plain.
It is no more than the intersection
of two volumes which find each other:
You can write and draw on it.

Volume is the surface in motion
outside itself through the perceived night.
By day it is the resistance of shadow.
Volume is no more than the intersection
of two complete times in one body:
Here we struggle and know, love and shut up.

translated by John Oliver Simon

UNTERGANG

An Karl Borromäus Heinrich

Georg
Trakl

Über den weissen Weiher
Sind die wilden Vögel fortgezogen.
Am Abend weht von unseren Sternen ein eisiger Wind.

Über unsere Gräber
Beugt sich die zerbrochene Stirne der Nacht.
Unter Eichen schaukeln wir auf einem silbernen Kahn.

Immer klingen die weissen Mauern der Stadt.
Unter Dornenbogen
O mein Bruder klimmen wir blinde Zeiger gen Mitternacht.

To Karl Borromäus Heinrich

Over the white pond   *Georg*
The wild birds have travelled on.   *Trakl*
In the evening an icy wind blows from our stars.

Over our graves
The broken brow of the night inclines.
Under oak trees we sway in a silver boat.

Always the town's white walls resound.
Under arches of thorns,
O my brother, blind minute-hands,
We climb towards midnight.

translated by Michael Hamburger

KLAGE

Georg
Trakl

Schlaf und Tod, die düstern Adler
Umrauschen nachtlang dieses Haupt:
Des Menschen goldnes Bildnis
Verschlänge die eisige Woge
Der Ewigkeit. An schaurigen Riffen
Zerschellt der pupurne Leib.
Und es klagt die dunkle Stimme
Über dem Meer.
Schwester stürmischer Schwermut
Sieh ein ängstlicher Kahn versinkt
Unter Sternen,
Dem schweigenden Antlitz der Nacht.

Sleep and death, the dark eagles   *Georg*
Around this head swoop all night long: *Trakl*
Eternity's icy wave
Would swallow the golden image
Of man; against horrible reefs
His purple body is shattered.
And the dark voice laments
Over the sea.
Sister of stormy sadness,
Look, a timorous boat goes down
Under stars,
The silent face of the night.

translated by Michael Hamburger

Tristan   by sea, transposed
Tzara   like a shot
              gun-shot
              finished
              who's your sister and who else
              under a glowing veil women saying tears are flowing
              boredom's atlantic
              what patience in the fickle crucibles
              before the muslin
              burning edges of speech
              ah forest-conjured and
                span
              ablason
              special and delicate papal death

translated by Yves Troendle

these two nerves that don't touch electric arc   *Tristan*
                       close to the heart   *Tzara*
              we verify the black shudder under a lens
is this feeling this white gushing
                   and methodical love
SPLIT MY BODY INTO RAYS
             toothpaste
              transatlantic squeeze box
the mob busts the wind-fucked pillar
rockets spread fanwise
          on my head
         bloody revenge of the liberated two-step
catalogue of pretensions at regular prices
                  madness at 3:20
         or 3 fr 50
cocaine slowly gnaws the walls for its enjoyment
             eyes are still falling

                 translated by Yves Troendle

Tristan
Tzara

we're going clouding with the eskimos
embellish the convalescence of our botanical ponderings
under twisted twilight
utter trash greening vibrant
whi

i've tidied up my inn-keeper candy-store commitments in his shop
definitive paulownias
the distances unravelling razor-sharp and glacial as diligence
the rainy distances
teen-age
noisy elsewhere

feverish rotten and gassed
out pedestrian with embroideries on the mend
i was just thinking of something filthy
in each tree an autumn calendar
my organ of love is blue
i'm mortal mr. blueblue

and from the corpse of a distant country rises
rises toward alien astronomies

translated by Yves Troendle

for: *Tristan*
mundane tea-parties   *Tzara*
matchbox-makers
money problems
a night of heavenly order
a nitric cylinder under a top-hat
a philosopher fallen into the thrill of virgin waterfalls
a lovely alpine countryside with a moon and rivulets deluxe
the cowboy roping us in with his lasso of talk
organ sugar
storm sugar
a missionary preaching insomnia
a glass foot full of water and birds
a nail pulled from fabulous fluids
the scorpion counting avalanches yet to come
and those avalanches carefully kept in postal bags by an
    anonymous company of soldiers with shiny taut skins now
    and then tumescent with our special product
"INTELLIGENCE"
the lowest-priced and longest-lasting
on sale
everywhere
always

translated by Yves Troendle

GREAT COMPLAINT AGAINST MY OBSCURITY III

Tristan
Tzara

where we come from, blossoms all over the clocks flare and
        feathers ring the light
cows lick their salt lilies in distant sulphur dawns
my son
my son

let's forever linger in the color of the world
you'd think a richer blue than subway or astronomy
we're much too skinny
we don't have any mouths
our legs are stiff our knees knock
like stars our faces have no shape
irrelevant crystal points scorched fire ah basilisk
gone nuts:
       lightning bolts
                                     like raw
telephone
to bite the ropes and liquefy
                                     flesh, fire
arc
to climb
                                     hunger
starry
memory
                                     blood
northbound by its own double fruit

translated by Yves Troendle

and what will ever replace it   *Hans*
                                                                                  Arp

wings fall from the table's peak
like earthen leaves
in front of lips
it's night inside the wings
the singing chains linking them are gone

the skeleton of light sucks the fruits

the body of kisses will never awaken
it was never real
the sea of wings lulls this tear
the bell talks with its head
the fingers drive us through fields of air
near nests full of eyes
the names are fading

and what will ever replace it
in the summits of the sky
nor sleep nor vigil
for tombs are brighter than days

translated by Yves Troendle

1

Douglas   Bring midnight in curses
Barbour   dead was man

when banished
tomb as book cried coxcomb

God like safety
black hunch stood solid

virginity bids all
wanders under other man

2

the thunder-stones storm heaven
great lover   fol

elaborate   adorning
delicate joints
heart roaring   rol

3

Love unsatisfied
take body   Jane

take me
I scold certainly

Naked   my hidden black Jane
can love be but said

4

meet bone
leave love   but dark

Douglas
Barbour

lonely come love's body
leap in

left empty
ghost head
night dead

5

lover came   went
I come   remain

Banners   men-at-arms   horses
battle in God

their childhood
uninhabited suddenly to all

wild like men
body sings all

6

I said   breasts   veins
live in

fair needs
friends denied bodily pride

proud love in excrement
nothing has

Douglas
Barbour

7

image chosen   wound
scream bodily under love

she said   strike fate   hate
love

die both
what limbs
dance love

8

I sing fancy   who
came   that upright   cried
was everything   young   old

9

change a heart
still rage beat

throw glances bravely
fade crone before

that heart knelt   all offended
pardon

10

beauty awaits love
best lesser prove

lovers breath touch
touch love   lie

11

love wrote of wrongs enough   undying
heart hard
know rock desolate leaps

12

Old kindred ever stood
that blood throws thin
what thorn has torn

*Douglas
Barbour*

13

dreamed fathomless
my love's but the night burning

14

Plato's set Eternity unwound
and loves   take thread
break thread
bargain all

15

give bone all pleasure of bone
          women sang bone
          body gave bone
think bone when rightful did bone

16

Beloved   you were
Paris   golden   dawn
such wild being
leap end run
as upon holy
accomplished Leda   protecting

17

speech estranged under night
again Art is ignorant

180

Douglas
Barbour

18

shutter foul minds
know everything mad

there below
page years unlettered   mist

makes me shudder
that   and snow

19

come   gone   that stone
body in the moon

sing what pleasure gave
sleeping   under
sun   moon

thought upon
man leans
until maid carry moon

20

Ireland and time come dance
        alone in man
        all stately is time   night
Ireland and time come dance
        fiddlers accursed   drums   trumpets
        and the malicious time
Ireland and time come dance

21

proclaiming men perfect
windy sang that cloud   proclaiming

22

sang under change
sight turned pure
and Holy
Wenching sing
something blinked in man
cock stands in faith

Douglas
Barbour

23

plain rhyme:
soul   Eternity
Time   world

24

perfection swelling
fail fantastic
            stormy winding-sheet

25

Behold seas
beckons Golden blood scattered
through there
            there
                    Love

Homolinguistic translation (one word per line)
of W.B Yeats's "Words for Music Perhaps."

The term *singularity* is borrowed from the lexicon of physics and the gravitational collapse. It is appropriate, applied to short pieces of writing so compact in effect that their logic is inescapable. The essence of *POLY* is diversity, and coiled at its heart is this expression of a poetic imperative toward the singular. Pared to the minimum, *POLY* is tumbling in upon itself, spiraling toward breath and brevity.

Ray Bradbury's early enthusiasm as reader and publisher, and his mature work as a writer helped bring science fiction to the world's attention. His reputation is secure in his superb short fiction, and his two s-f novels *Fahrenheit 451* and *Something Wicked This Way Comes*. Less well known are the many *Twilight Zone* episodes he authored, his design work at the 1960 New York World's Fair, and remarkably, a lunar crater, *Dandelion*, named in his honor. Still exploring, he has recently published a mystery novel. Here he starts *POLY*'s engine of compression with the couplets of "To Ireland, No More..." in print for the first time.

Michael Hamburger continues the process with "On Duty," a dream-poem new for *POLY*, located in disturbingly familiar terrain. His poems have appeared in the Penguin Modern Poets series, and in his books *Flowering Cactus* (1950), *Poems 1950–1951* (1952), *The Dual Site* (1958), *Weather and Season* (1963), *Ownerless Earth* (1973), *Real Estate* (1977), *Moralities* (1977), *Variations* (1981), and the three *Travelling* books (1969, 1973, 1975).

Widely published Steve Rasnic Tem was editor of the 1982 collection *The Umbral Anthology of Science Fiction Poetry*. "Looking Back on Apollo" is his sombre celebration of the best-known event of our era.

Next, Mark Rich leads into more distant regions with a new poem "To The Colony." Co-editor of *Treaders of Starlight* from 1974 to 1976, and of *The Magazine of Speculative Poetry* since 1984, he lives in Wisconsin, and has published in *Uranus*, *Star*Line*, *Fantasy Review*, *Visions*, and *Pandora*.

Toronto's Yves Troendle is author of two novels from Oolichen Press, *Journey to the Sun* (1978), and *Raven's Children* (1980). His poems have been published in *Kayak*, *Poetry Canada Review*, *Zest*, *Industrial Sabotage*, and the *Toronto Connection anthology*. In "Moon," he compresses a considerable surreal cosmology into one telling.

Finally, Mark Laba, sometime dishwasher, insulation salesman, watch assembler, and contributor to *Industrial Sabotage*, sums up with a statement from which all the fat has been boiled. Much in the style of his impeccable 1-cent-to-1-dollar singlesheet poems, *Card #27* is reprinted from a Curvd H&Z limited edition (1983).

I dare not go — that land has ghosts

Ray
Bradbury

And spectral rains along the coasts
Such rains as weep their loss in tears
Till I am drowned in sunken years.
When last I walked a Dublin street,
My gaze was clear, my pulses fleet,
Now half a life or more is gone
I cannot face sad Dublin's dawn.
The book clerks who once waited me
Are grey and gaunt, how can that be?
The hotel staff has up and fled,
Some stay as haunts, the rest are dead.
The candy butchers, beggars, maids,
Sleep out beyond in Meynooth's shades,
O'Connell's harpists? gone to stay
Deep strewn along the hills at Bray.
Their happy faces smoke and stream
Across my life to shape each dream
So, Ireland? No, I'll not return
Where ghosts in smoking rainfalls burn.
Through Dublin I'll not stroll again
I cannot stand that haunted rain
Where youngness melts away to sea
And kills my soul, my heart, and me.

Written enroute from Palm Springs
Monday afternoon/12:05 to 12:10 p.m.
March 1, 1983

Michael
Hamburger

Attending the telephone
I take to be still connected
To some headquarters or other
Become expert in reticence,
I try to remember the old war
I joined up for, but can't get beyond
The trestle bed I rose from
This morning, any morning
In a barrack room shared with no one;
And can't be sure when it was
That a bugle inside my head,
Blowing reveille, became
The blare that roused me from nightmare
At the moment of sudden awareness
That years or decades have passed
Since my parents answered a letter,
Of the flash in darkness showing me
The girl I was to have married
Smile to herself undecided
Between two bedroom doors,
Each with a man behind it.
Awake, must ask myself,
Man? Is the designation current?
If ever again a voice
Should come through, will it use
Human, obsolete words
To charge, discharge me
Whose number, rank, name
Were dropped long ago
From records transferred to computers,
And leave this table real,
This pen, the blank forms?

Or is silence not only the code
but the message I'm here to receive
And pass on, undeciphered?
Pass on to whom, though, to whom?

Steve
Rasnic Tem

That first step:
rising on belief, virtuosity,
and the dreamed moon encounters
arcane yet real locomotion.

A step out of old compromise
where gravity bargained with our dance,
a step away from adamant pavement
where twisted legs and unease
were the body's torquing against the upright
and the mind translating its bearings.

Into the light and deep shadow
under a sky blown away,
a first step, almost a leap—
that one bounce and we wanted to keep going
to find our heart's center in the stars.

We walk into solitude not felt
since the first animal eye,
but never before
had we such evolution.

Mark
Rich

Ship-pod has burst
and we float, autumn-winged.
Before re-timing instinct,
refitting, rethinking,
we walked with the ease
we now catch gust and turn
sweeping sight from morning to night.
I used to lift arms pretending patterned wings
lulled me into air, a buoyed hope,
and I would say to the gang, Jimmy and Bets,
"They'll put them on there, and there,"
and we would tumble down park green slope,
invisible dragonfly vanes lifting
into October leaves
winged red on their own invisible purposes;
wind releases and relieves
attachment from tree to world.
We suspend memories now
in this drift down to our floating home,
there where we will rest and leave
all older wings furled.

When she was a girl, coming home across a field, an owl followed her. She
couldn't see it because the sun was out, but she smelled it in the crushed
grass and the nests of mice, and heard the heavy wet sheets thudding in the
wind. Then every night she saw it beating its wings over her bed, the soft
white feathers raining around her. When she arched her spine and clutched
the bed-posts, she felt the wood crumble in her grip. Then the owl would
disappear, fusing with dawn, and she'd run to the window and watch the
clouds bloom into light, and death nibble at the edges of the sky.

When the owl no longer came, she locked herself in and waited. She locked
herself out and looked and looked. She saw the whole neighborhood
gathered in the street, clubbing the owl as it rolled around in fury, but when
she ran up weeping, nobody was there—all the houses cast shadows that
yawned. She wandered all night. Everywhere she stepped she woke a star
into shining.

Everything she shines on gives up its color, questions its shape.

Yves
Troendle

Mark
Laba

You monster sacrificing yourself to a mountain of glass,
you're not immortal, just a yellow jewel of blood

lives on the Isle of Wight. In 1932 at age sixteen, he published a novel and a book of poems and spent the proceeds getting to France and among the surrealists. His *Journal de Paris & d'ailleurs, 1937–1942* (Flammarion 1984) is full of personal recollections of Tzara, Auden, Valery, Cocteau, Andre Breton. His books include *Man's Life is his Meat* (Parton Press 1936), *Holderlin's Madness* (J.M. Dent & Sons 1938), *Poems 1937–1942* (Nicholas & Watson 1943), *A Vagrant & Other Poems* (John Lehman 1950), *Night Thoughts* (Andre Deutsch 1955), *Collected Poems* (Oxford University Press 1965), and *Collected Verse Translations* (Oxford University Press 1970).

Gascoyne's *Procession to the Private Sector* is a major work, a surrealist film scenario written in the nineteen thirties and heretofore published only in France, in Michel Remy's study *David Gascoyne ou l'urgence de l'inexprime*. A newly corrected *Procession* now appears in *POLY* in its first anglophone edition.

PROCESSION TO THE PRIVATE SECTOR
Surrealist film scenario 1936—1982

David
Gascoyne

FOREWORD

It is difficult to give a *précis* of a surrealist film. Originally written in the mid-thirties, when I was still an accredited member of the surrealist movement, in Paris as well as in London, it was to have been called "The Wrong Procession." I gave it the updated title in 1981, when rewriting the scenario from a photocopy of the Ms now in the British (Museum) Library.

The subject-matter of the film derives, at least in part, from an authentic dream, which rightly or wrongly I considered at the time to be of collective as well as individual import. The stylized "battle-scene" which constitutes the centre-piece of the film is not so much an anticipation of World War II, which at that time was beginning to seem inevitable, as a reflection of "the class-struggle," or rather the conflict between the progressive and the reactionary forces in society. The story-line, in so far as there is one, concerns the vicissitudes of an amorous couple: the young "protagonist" and his female counterpart, both intended as minimally personalized stereotypes. There are only two subsidiary characters of any importance; the rest of the cast consists of two initially contrasting groups of as many people as are needed to create the impression of a crowd. A modern dance group, or two working in collaboration, would be ideal, as their movements at certain moments ought to be choreographed. The key symbol in the second half is obviously sexual, but stands primarily for an ideological "key to the problem of the world-crisis situation," which the "protagonist"—representing the romantic liberal idealist "in extremis"—deludedly imagines to have been entrusted to him.

The author believes that many second-rate, banal but popular films often embody myths of authentic importance, which satisfy audiences which appreciate subliminally their possibly unintentional socio-psychoanalytic content. The ideas behind this film are now perceived by the author as serious, and possibly more pessimistic than he would have intended at the time of its conception. It is not, however, intended to be seen as solemn propaganda, but primarily to entertain on the level of fantasy. It contains elements of parody and send-up, as well as what may be considered a symptomatic reflection of 20th century man's essential dilemma and quest.

David Gascoyne, Spring 1984

AUTHOR'S NOTE

This scenario was originally written in the mid-thirties in a notebook now belonging to the British (Museum) Library. From a photocopy, I have now revised and corrected it, incidentally making it slightly more up-to-date than the first draft. Notes in the margin of the Ms suggest that I had originally intended a surrealist-type poem to be incorporated as spoken commentary at a certain juncture; but I do not think I was ever able to produce a poetic text suitable for this purpose. As I am no longer capable of producing the type of poem that might be appropriate, I have selected three short texts (by Wittegenstein, Rimbaud and Nietzsche respectively) that a putative director could use should he consider they add interest to the film by clarifying what is for me its underlying significance, or leave out were he to decide that they would tend to create too portentous an impression. I have labelled the texts I have chosen *Voice Over's*, and added them to the scenario as an appendix. I should like to complete this note by quoting two passages from Nicolas Berdyaev's "Towards a New Epoch" (1949), which in combination seem to me to encapsulate the underlying implication of the film as I dimly saw it at the end of its first conception, and to be at present even more relevant to what I should hope the film to be thought of as fundamentally about than I could have planned when I first outlined it:

David
Gascoyne

The theme of liberty is tragic, particularly for the cultural elite, which is passing through a serious crisis. If this elite is not penetrated through and through by the idea of service, if it remains imprisoned in self-satisfaction, despising those beneath itself, it will be condemned to disappear. Whatever may be the upshot the liberalism of the eighteenth and nineteenth centuries is finished and from now onwards impotent. The individualism which in former times was capable of being revolutionary has become nothing but a fruitless regret for the past. Economic liberalism particularly is becoming a reactionary force, the prop of capitalism at its last ebb. Liberal democracy is again equally played out. Attempts are, of course, made to keep it going, but it is an obstacle in the way of the social reform of society.

The future should not be conceived as if it were to be integrated and unified. It will always present us with a duality and spiritual conflict. This will doubtless be particularly acute when the social struggle is over. Then the spiritual problem, at present concealed beneath social disorders and contradictions, will come to the fore in its pure state.

David Gascoyne, May 1982

Surrealist film scenario

Suggested Musical Background:
—Arnold Schönberg: "Music for a Film Scene"
—Alban Berg: Movement from "Lyric Suite"
—Edgar Varèse: "Ionisation"

David
Gascoyne

The title and credits are superimposed on a background shot of rising clouds of heavy smoke, accompanied by a high-pitched whistle-note, which fades away and stops at the moment the titles end. The shot of smoke then dissolves into one of a long uphill street of suburban villas seen in the half-light of early morning. Beginning of music.

— A head lying on a crumpled pillow. At first only the mouth is seen. It gradually opens wide. The entire face is slowly revealed: it is that of a young man, with widely opened eyes and anguished expression, who appears to have just awoken from a nightmare. He rubs his eyes and turns to stare at the drawn window-curtains of a dingy, untidy room. Early morning light is beginning to penetrate them. The young man jumps out of bed and hurriedly starts to get dressed.

— Long-shot from the bedroom-window. The long deserted street. No-one in sight but a postman a few doors away. Shot of the front door of the house in which the young man has just awakened. Then the postman is seen approaching. He inserts a postcard into the letter-box, knocks hard and goes away.

— The top of the staircase. The young man emerges from the bedroom-door and hurries down the stairs, pulling on his jacket and straightening his tie as he goes. His hair is still disheveled. He takes the postcard from the door and reads it. At first an expression of shocked dismay crosses his face, he claps a hand to his brow; then he begins to smile increasingly and ends by rocking with laughter.

— Close-up of the words written on the postcard: *Your home has been burnt to the ground and your wife is in the arms of a stranger:*
THE TRAIN LEAVES AT 8:30 A.M.

Still laughing, the young man puts the postcard into his pocket, shaking his head. He then immediately takes his hat and coat from the hall rack, puts them on, and hastily exits through the front-door, which he slams to behind him.

The next shot is of the garden-fence in front of one of the neighbouring houses, behind which an unshaven individual of brutal appearance is shown hiding. As the young man steps onto the pavement, this person emerges from his hiding-place and advances up the road to confront him. He is seen to be wearing some kind of black uniform. Without a word of warning, he knocks the young man to the ground with a punch on the jaw, kicks him, then runs away leaving him sprawled in the gutter.

The young man lying motionless at the edge of the road, a thread of blood running down his chin. Dissolve into shot of uprising smoke, as at the beginning.

Superimposed on the smoke, the following words:
YOUR HOME HAS BEEN BURNT TO THE GROUND...

Smoke fades into a shot of a desolate piece of wasteland. In the foreground, a few scattered heaps of bricks covered with cinders and ash, some old clothes still burning, are lying about among newspapers and books and a miscellaneous debris of bric-a-brac. At the centre of the muddle stand a brokendown wicker chair still in flames and beside it a three-legged table supporting a small glass globe containing goldfish. From the misty distance, an old woman with her head covered by a black shawl and carrying a black umbrella advances towards the camera. Her clothing is shown to be covered with patches of white flour or powder. She hobbles up to the table and smashes the goldfishbowl with her umbrella. The fish lie on the stoney ground, wriggling among the ashes.

Further dissolve into rising smoke, superimposed with the words:
...AND YOUR WIFE...

This time the smoke dissolves into a different interior. In it the old woman is seen again, with the back of her shawled head facing the camera. After a pause, she turns round, straightens up and throws off the shawl, revealing a beautiful, young and laughing blonde. Close-up of her face.

Dissolve into close-up of the (dark) back of a sofa. Superimposed on this background appear the words:
...IS IN THE ARMS OF A STRANGER.

The camera now pans round to confront the sofa. On it the young woman is seen going through the motions of making love with an invisible character. In doing so, she mimes a parody of the erotic contortions typical of an X movie, while avoiding as far as possible the appearance of indulging in "solitary pleasure." Her lips move, the expression of her face becomes ecstatic, she seems to be frantically caressing someone else. While this is happening, several eggs fall down, apparently from the ceiling, to break on the floor surrounding the sofa. She is too engrossed in her passionate activity with an unseen partner to pay any attention to this happening.

Exploratory shot of the room surrounding the young woman. It is a conventionally furnished sitting-room, with open fireplace surmounted by a mantlepiece on which to one side of the clock stands an ornately-framed wedding photograph of the young woman holding a bouquet and the hand of the man seen in the opening sequence. A close-up of the broken eggs on the floor is followed by one of the young woman's now swooning face, which dissolves into the face of the mantlepiece clock: the hands mark 8:25.

The door of the room, seen for about 30 seconds before it bursts open to admit a group of a dozen or so drunken revellers in evening dress, wearing paper hats, false noses, dominoes, etc., and festooned with paper streamers. They rush wildly about the room, overturning articles of furniture, breaking vases and fighting one another. Among them, though he should not be immediately recognizable, is the character last seen lying in the gutter. The woman on the sofa appears to remain oblivious of the action taking place around her; she resumes caressing her invisible lover.

Second close-up of the clock-face: its hands have moved five minutes forward. Shot moves slowly up to the mirror above it. On its surface have been written with chalk or lipstick the words:

THE TRAIN LEAVES AT 8:30.

The disorderly intruders suddenly appear to become aware of the time, looking anxiously at the clock, nudging each other and consulting their wristwatches. The camera now focuses on the young man of the opening scene. In a state of evident agitation, he rushes to the sofa and starts tugging the woman's arm. She thereupon gives a violent start and appears to awaken as though from a trance.

—The revellers are now all rushing out of the room, followed by the principal man, dragging his supposed "wife," whose face expresses dazed astonishment, after him. Last shot of the empty room, the door left open.

— A wide dimly-lit staircase, down which a confused heard of people are stampeding.

— Now follows a sequence of rapid, scrambled shots.—The revellers running down a street at accelerated speed.—Closeups of frantic, perspiring faces; running feet and legs. Revolving trainwheels. Traffic and railway signals. Intermittent clouds of smoke or steam. Blurred shots of clocks on public buildings. Postered walls rushing past.

— Shot of a railway-platform, with a train first immobile, then beginning to leave.

— Revert to further shot of the group of people rushing through the streets.

— The empty station platform.

— The rushing crowd once more. Some of its members collapse in exhaustion, to be trampled underfoot.

— Shot of a train travelling at full speed through an open countryside.

Repeat last shot of rushing crowd. Dissolve into shot of the facade of a Victorian Gothic redbrick railway-station. Camera swings to record the arrival into the forecourt of the small gasping, panic-stricken crowd.

David
Gascoyne

— The station doors surmounted by an ENTRANCE sign. The next shot shows the same doors as seen from inside the station. They are violently pushed open and in rush the already disheveled travellers, followed by the protagonist, dragging his fainting ''wife'' after him with difficulty. Focus on the torn, stained, disordered appearance of the group's clothing, then on their wild, perspiring faces. Their expressions of anxiety abruptly change to looks of surprised astonishment and a different kind of alarm, as they gaze around them: What a strange building they are now in!

— Exploratory shots disclose an enormous, empty interior resembling a hangar, gymnasium or skating-rink, its lofty roof supported by metal scaffolding and rafters. At the far end of this hall, first shown in long-shot and then slowly approached, is to be seen standing a long trestle table, around and upon which is discovered a new group, or team, of curiously attired people. Their attitudes are grotesquely unconventional; some of them are lying on the table, some on the floor, some lying or kneeling on top of the others. Others are standing, some leaning to one side, with arms and legs twisted or stretched out wide. All are either wearing masks or have their faces painted white like clowns. Some of them are naked except for a pair of briefs; others are dressed in some sort of uniform, in particular the loutish individual previously seen committing an assault on the protagonist earlier in the film. Some are draped in flags, some wearing cloaks, some are wearing tea-cosies on their heads; while a few of the women are attired in Victorian fashion or nun's habits. Among them are what appear to be a priest, an admiral and a general; one is a gentleman sporting a frock-coat, top-hat and spats. All are at first shown perfectly motionless, like a group of statuary, during a shot lasting at least 30 seconds.

— The next shot is of the travellers at the opposite end of the hall, all of them apparently overcome with horror and consternation. At first, some of them are seen to be attempting to escape, but they discover the doors to be locked. The hall is devoid of windows. All of the members of this group next start to cower back against the wall behind them, and in so doing manage to upset a few of the baskets of flowers, fruit and other edibles that have been arranged at their end of the hall.

— Focus reverts to the motionless group opposite the travellers, at first in longshot, then after gradual panning towards them, in close-up. After a moment, all their faces begin to twitch rapidly and to display idiotic grimaces; then are abruptly frozen into immobility.

— Long-shot once more from the travellers' end of the hall. A figure among the group facing them emerges from his companions. He is dressed in sports-jacket and and flannel trousers; over his head he is wearing a sort of sack or cushion-cover in which two slits have been pierced for the eyes. He runs swiftly and gracefully to the exact centre of the hall, where he sinks on one knee, his arms

stiffly extended level with his shoulders. He is followed by two other represen-
tatives of his "team" who are carrying a large placard between them, which they
solemnly hold behind the kneeling figure's head.

— Close-up of the sack-masked head and of the placard behind it, on which
are legible the words:

MAKE WAR NOT LOVE!

— Focus reverts to the revellers/travellers, and settles on the "wife" of the pro-
tagonist. An expression of delighted surprise, quickly verging on ecstasy,
transforms her face. Without hesitation, she rushes forward, flings her arms round
the half-kneeling, motionless figure in front of the placard and attempts t embrace
him. He remains with arms rigidly outstretched, then abruptly shakes her off with
such violence that she falls back on to the floor. Behind him, the two placard-
bearers change places, thus revealing the other side of the notice, on which is
written:

THIS MEANS WAR!

— At this point, the statuesque group of figures at the far end of the hall comes
to life and starts to prepare for the opening of hostilities. From behind the trestle
table on and around which they have been posed, they begin to lift and expose
to view on the table-top a previously concealed arsenal of miscellaneous articles:
An alarm-clock, tins of sardines, rolls of paper, a shooting-stick, a violin, a crucifix,
photograph-albums, plaster busts of famous composers, gloves, a frying-pan,
chess-pieces, a transistor, a rubic cube, plastic dolls, a weighing-machine, garden
tools, bones, cups and saucers, coat-hangars, gold-balls, etc., etc. The placard-
bearers have meanwhile turned, put the placard away under the table and taken
out another, which they now proceed to carry forward and display to the oppos-
ing side. It reads:

WAR IS NOW INEVITABLE!

— The motley figures now start to fling their objects one after another into the
centre of the hall.

— The protagonist's followers realize they must reply to this assault, and turn
to pick up from the ground behind them handfuls of the flowers, fruit and vegetables
they had scattered from the baskets that were standing at their end at the outset.

— Focus is now directed on the previously kneeling figure with a sack over
his head. He springs up, takes a whistle from his pocket and starts to run about
among the melee like a referee. The opposing groups rush at one another without
restraint, throwing incongruous missiles in all directions. A situation of utter con-
fusion and increasing violence ensues. Details of the struggle to be picked out
momentarily by the camera include:

— A figure wearing a pigtail, which repeatedly gets pulled by his opponents. — A nursemaid rushing about with a pram full of empty milk-bottles. — An elegantly dressed elderly woman with white hair, who after persistent attempts to observe what is taking place about her through a lorgnette, while being pushed from side to side, finally gets knocked down and trampled on. — The referee constantly consulting his wristwatch. — Struggling couples on top of one another here and there. — A figure scattering confetti; another occupied in sprinkling the fallen with a large watering-can.

— Meanwhile, the faithless "wife" is rushing about in every direction, continually attempting to embrace all and sundry and each time encountering a brusque rebuff.

— Throughout this scene, constituting for the most part a "master shot," particular attention should be paid to the "protagonist" figure who, when not trying to prevent his "wife" from embracing their enemies, is chiefly engaged in dodging the loutish uniformed character who has previously attacked him and who now persists in chasing him from corner to corner of the set, armed with a dangerous-looking club. The scene should be rhythmically intercut with a number of apparently quite irrelevant shots: A fireworks display; a flying helicopter; the demolition of a building; armed guerrillas alongside corpses; carnivores in a zoo; one or two minimal extracts of footage from TV commercials such as "Black Magic"; etc.

— By the conclusion of the preceding scene, all the participants are lying struggling with one another convulsively on the floor, and a state of chaos has been attained. Damaged or shattered heterogeneous objects are strewn about the writing bodies. All movement is decelerated into immobility, while the musical accompaniment simultaneously diminishes into silence. For the first time the voice of the "protagonist" is heard:

"Is the end of the world at hand?"

As he utters these words, an enormous sheet of gauze or muslin is shown floating slowly down from the roof, until finally it envelopes the now motionless muddle on the ground entirely. Freeze for approximately 30 seconds.

— Dissolve, into a similar shot showing the same sheet of gauze/muslin covering a heap of bodies and objects, the shape of which must look as much as possible the same as at the conclusion of the previous scene. As the following shot recedes from the covered heap, the surroundings are revealed as having changed. They have in fact become the misty and derelict piece of wasteland on which the earlier scene of the site of the supposed remains of a burnt home was shot. Next, feeble movement is shown disturbing the gauze. Gradually the disturbance travels towards the edge of the diaphanous cover, and finally the "protagonist" emerges from beneath it. He is evidently in pain and looks in every way worse for wear. He begins closely to examine the stoney ground, on which a few derelict items of rubbish remain strewn. At last he discovers an unusually large, rusty-looking key fastened to the end of a long chain. He picks it up, giving the impression that it is unusually heavy; and the following shot shows him slowly trudging away towards the distance, dragging it after him as the end of its chain.

— Brief frozen frame of the finally deserted landscape.

— Dissolve into long shot of an apparently endless corridor. Then the "protagonist" appears in the foreground, and is next seen receding down the corridor, dragging the key behind him.

— The next shot explores a typical hotel entrance-lounge, focusing finally on an elderly white-moustached gentleman seated in an armchair and reading a newspaper. Swing toward a curtained archway at far end of set. The curtain is pushed aside, and the young man with a key emerges, looking anxious and down-and-out. He hesitantly approaches the hotel resident, carrying the cumbersome key and its chain in his hands. Then he leans over the old man's chair from one side, as though intending to address a question to him. The old man lowers his paper with a start, sits up to scrutinize the interloper and assumes an expression of outraged fury. The "protagonist" holds out the key and chain towards him beseechingly, as though proffering an explanation of his intrusion. The old man's anger at once increases, he rolls up his newspaper and brandishes it with one hand at his interlocutor, while pointing with the other imperiously to the swing-doored entrance. After increased entreaty and correspondingly furious remonstrance between the two characters, the young man makes a disappointed retreat towards the entrance.

— There follows a brief episode involving the hotel swingdoors which should be treated in traditional burlesque manner. The attempted exit of the young man with the key, now in his hands and trailing its chain, is thwarted by the determined entry of someone from outside. Shot alternately from inside and outside the doors, the young man and the new entrant are shown engaged in increasingly desperate contest to get through the doors, one in, one out, hampered by the entanglement of the keychain in the doors' central hinge. This is finally resolved by the young man's emerging in obvious discomfiture into a busy street.

— Shot of the street, as seen from the kerbside about 50 yards from the hotel entrance, recognizable from the sign hanging above it: IMPERIAL HOTEL. The young man is seen tottering out on to the pavement, dragging the key he has succeeded in extricating from the revolving door. In the foreground, a young woman in smart attire is bending to pay attention to one of her shoes which is giving her trouble, incidentally displaying provocative portions of her anatomy. The young man is seen approaching her, his face wearing an expression of re-signed disillusionment. She straightens up as he reaches her side, whereupon he proffers her the key. With a furious look of incredulous scorn, she slaps his face forcefully and hastens away towards the hotel. Holding the key pressed to his chest and trailing its chain, the "protagonist" shrugs his shoulders and wanders sadly off out of sight in the other direction.

— The next shot reveals a stone bridge of medium size. The young man appears, slowly advancing from one end towards the middle. When he has reached it, he starts to fasten the chain he had been dragging around his neck: he then dangles the key over the balustrade. It becomes apparent that he is about to throw himself into the river beneath. Camera now swings to focus on the other end of the bridge, where the figure of a policeman is visible. As soon as he observes what the young man is doing, he comes racing towards him. He claps his hand on the would-be suicide's shoulder, shaking his head angrily; then, after a brief demonstration of remonstrance, he moves away in the direction of the end of the bridge at which the young man first appeared, holding his hands behind his back. The young man begins to move slowly in the other direction, dragging the key behind him again, his expression blank.

— The following scene represents a street-corner meeting. The young man with the key is seen approaching a crowd of people grouped round an orator who is haranguing them from a small rostrum draped with the Union Jack. The speaker is wearing a variety of medals and decorations and has a cleric's collar; his face is distorted and he is making increasingly impassioned arm-movements. The young man joins the outer fringe of the crowd and stands there listlessly for a while, trying to hear the speech. As he listens, he becomes visibly angry and indignant. Finally, his patience at an end, he takes up the key with both hands, unfastens it from its chain, and casts it with all his might at the speaker. It falls heavily to the ground at the speaker's feet, causing no damage, without even interrupting the oration. The members of the crowd pay no attention to the incident, with the exception of one business-suited individual who, having carefully picked up the missile, turns around and having without apparent difficulty identified its thrower, makes his way over to him and politely hands it back. With an expression of wretched resignation, the young man refastens the key to its chain and, dragging it behind him again, slowly leaves the scene.

Now ensues a sequence of street-scenes, each featuring the young man dragging his key behind him at the end of its chain. Three or four medium-range shots, of relatively brief duration, each showing a different, progressively less populated street, should be sufficient. In each the "protagonist" will be seen slowly making his way, a lonely and incongruous figure, among pedestrians hurrying past without paying him any attention.

— The next shot after this peregrination sequence shows us a nondescript place on the outskirts of the town. The most outstanding feature of the shabby landscape is a high brick wall appearing to separate unkempt allotments from open wasteland. Zoom in on the wall to show, positioned against it, an elderly man with a long, bushy white beard, wearing a skull cap. He is apparently engaged in trying clumsily to lop off his beard with a pair of shears. (If a wall can be found with the creeping plant known as "old-man's-beard" growing on it, the visual pun would considerably enhance the effect of this incident.) On the ground beside the old man lies a very large, awkwardly shaped brown-paper parcel; it is intricately tied-up with string and cords. The size and shape of the parcel, and the fact that it momentarily jerks from side to side, suggest that it contains a living human body.

— The camera now swings to the left to record the shambling approach of the young man trailing his key from the direction of the nearby towns. Then, it swings to the right, showing the old man cutting off his beard for a passing instant before fixing on the simultaneous approach from elsewhere of the young "wife," or "heroine," of earlier scenes. She is now clad in a swim-suit or bikini, and carries a beach-bag. The young man with the key greets her, she smiles dreamily, and they embrace with visible emotion. They then stand hand in hand, watching the eccentric activity of the old man at the foot of the wall for a while. He continues lopping off hanks of his beard, and now as he is doing so the young woman steps forward, stoops down, gathers up the scattered bits of shorn beard lying on the ground and stuffs them into her bag. As she does so, the mystery parcel at the old man's side begins to move convulsively, but the couple pay not the slightest attention to this phenomenon, of which they appear oblivious. Finally, having embraced once more, they go off together, without having addressed a word to the old man, the young man with his arm about his "wife's" shoulders. They are walking along the wall away from the town.

— The following shot returns briefly to the old man, who by this time has nearly divested himself of his beard. He now turns to the mysterious parcel beside him and with shears he has been using, cuts through the complicated entanglement of cords and string containing it; whereupon the personage concealed within bursts through the paper and reveals himself as an individual wearing black trousers, an open-necked white shirt and a domino mask, armed with a revolver. Facing the old but now beardless man who has released him, he gives him a military salute, turns abruptly on his heel and bounds off in immediate pursuit of the departed couple, as fast as possible. The closing shot of this scene shows him from the rear, disappearing into the (blurred) distance.

— Dissolve into medium shot showing the reunited couple making their way along the foot of the wall, the young man dragging his key at the end of its chain behind him. Before long, they reach a massive door set in an archway in the wall. The door has a conspicuous keyhole. The young man detaches his key from its chain and approaches the door with it, applying it to the keyhole. Consternation: it is far too big to fit the hole. In exasperation, the young man drops the key. He is then seen looking down at it on the ground. Close-up of the key: it has noticeably diminished in size. The "protagonist" then picks it up again with an astonished expression. He once more tries to fit it into the keyhole, but it is still too large.

He at once drops it again. Second close-up of the key. Its fall has again made it smaller. A further attempt is made to fit the key to the lock, only once more to meet frustration. A slow zoom in on the key on the ground now reveals it to be of normal size. The young man picks it up, fits it into the lock, turns it and triumphantly pushes the heavy door wide open. The couple pass through the doorway together, hand in hand, leaving the key in the lock and the door ajar.

— Shot of the back side of the wall, in close-up. On it gradually appear the superimposed words: THE ISLAND WAS COMPLETELY DESERTED.

— Long-shot of the couple crossing a wide stretch of open country. In the distance, a few factory chimneys and a gasworks are dimly discernible. Dusk is falling. The next shot discloses the edge of a gloomy wood, which the couple are approaching.

— The couple are next shown entering the wood and discovering with difficulty a narrow pathway through the trees. Dim lighting.

— The next shot zooms in to focus on a tree about fifteen yards further along and to the side of the path the couple are following. Shot shifts to the back of the tree, revealing the masked figure with a revolver seen previously being released from a mysterious parcel. This personage is now evidently in ambush. Shot returns to the couple advancing along the path. Intensify lighting. At the moment they reach the point on the path alongside which stands the tree concealing their would-be assailant, he steps into view, his revolver aimed at the couple. Close-up of the mouth of the weapon. Then of their shocked faces. Medium shot of the young man putting an arm round his companion's shoulders. The threatened pair stand perfectly still, while their faces assume an expression of complete calm. (At this point, the Voice over quotation from Wittgenstein could begin, read slowly and distinctly in a neutral tone.) As they stand staring unafraid at the masked figure, he slowly approaches them, his revolver ready to fire. At the moment he has reached lethally close range, the young woman suddenly lies down flat on her back in front of him. The young man then deliberately places one foot on her abdomen, at the same moment stretching out his arm at full length, directing an accusing forefinger at the weapon. Frame of the confrontation briefly frozen. Next, the menacing figure is seen to rip off his mask, revealing the face of the "unshaven individual of brutal appearance" who featured in one of the opening sequences of the film. His visage now wears an expression of superstitious terror. He starts back, points his revolver to his own temple and fires. Half way through his fall to the ground, shot in slow motion, his body totally disappears.

— The next shots show the couple resuming their slow advance along the path through the wood. The lighting has become dim again, as before the hallucinatory murder-threat episode. As they move forward, various figures are seen to step one by one from behind trees on either side of the path, and to begin to follow them, gradually forming a procession. They should be recognizably the same as the "revellers" or thwarted "travellers" who took part in earlier scenes. Finally, when the cast of the cortege has completely assembled, they all emerge from the obscurity of the wood, led by the young man and his companion. They are now seen to be wearing clothing that is similar, sober and simple. They are confronted by a further stretch of open twilit countryside.

— (At this point, if it is used, the Voice Over reading of a translation of the last paragraph of section IV of Rimbaud's *Enfance* should begin, this time by a different, younger voice.)

— The footpath through the wood continues through the country beyond it into the distance. On either side of it the camera, when not recording the slow progress of the procession, picks out details such as heaps of weedgrown stones, empty bottles, rusting cans, broken toys, an abandoned car chassis. From time to time, what appears to be a sprawling corpse left behind in this no-man's-land comes to life and totteringly joins the tail-end of the procession.

— At this point, the camera must focus for a time on the path, to show that it has by now become a disused railway-track, with grass and wild-flowers sprouting between the lines (this flora should, if possible, include a clump of the broom, or gorse, mentioned in the Rimbaud poem quotation). The ground ahead is now seen to be sloping increasingly upward, till it reaches a quite steep gradient. The members of the procession have assumed the semblance of a team of explorers, struggling on doggedly towards some unknown goal, weary and worn but comradely. Some have joined hands, others are leaning on companions' shoulders. They persist in following the railway-track to the brow of the hill. At the top, against the skyline, a tattered flag hung from a broken pole, is to be seen.

— A sequence of concluding shots now show: first, the leading couple, he with his arms around his beloved's neck, their faces serene; next, one after the other, the companions who have rejoined them; and lastly, the resuscitated victims, in bloody and ragged clothes, who have joined the procession at the last moment. They are then seen from the rear, passing one by one over the brow of the hill and out of sight.

— Long shot of the empty, disused railway-track leading uphill, the tattered flag, the dim ray sky beyond. Then, as the film closes, the sky begins to glow with radiant orange light. (If the Voice Over extract from Nietzsche is used, a voice should recite it as the glow begins and increases.) As the last shot fades, a distant echo of the high-pitched whistle with which the film opened should be heard.

*(Possible Voice Over texts from Wittgenstein,
Rimbaud and Nietzsche appended.)*

*David
Gascoyne*

"If someone says, only the *present experience* has reality, then the word 'present' must be redundant here, as the word 'I' is in other contexts. For it cannot mean *present* as opposed to past and future.— Something else must be meant by the word, something that isn't *in* a space, but is itself a space. That is to say, not something bordering on something else (from which it could therefore be limited off). And so, something language cannot legitimately set in relief.

"The present we are talking about here is not the frame in the film reel that is in front of the projector's lens at precisely this moment, as opposed to the frames before and after it, which have already been there or are yet to come; but the picture on the screen which would illegitimately be called present, since 'present' would not be used here to distinguish it from past and future. And so it is not a meaningless epithet."

Ludwig Wittgenstein (Philosophical Remarks)

II. VOICE OVER

"The flag makes its way to the foul landscape, and our jabber drowns the sound of drums.

"In the town-centres we shall maintain the most cynical prostitution. We shall repress logical revolts with slaughter.

"To the syphilized and softened lands! — in the service of the most monstrous industrial or military exploitations.

"Good-bye to here, no matter where. Conscripts to good-will, ours will be a ferocious philosophy: uninformed with regard to science, shrewd whenever comfort is concerned; bust-up for the world in progress. That's true advance. Forward, march!"

*Arthur Rimbaud
(Translation from* Democratie, *nº 37 in* Illuminations.*)*

(To precede or replace the above)

"The tracks are rugged. The hillocks are covered in broom. How far off are the birds and the springheads! This can only be the end of the world approaching."

*Arthur Rimbaud
(From the end of* Enfance, IV, *nº 2 of* Illuminations.*)*

"— The real world — unattainable? Unattained, at any rate. And if unattained also *unknown*. Consequently also no consolation, no redemption, no duty; how could we have a duty towards something unknown?

"(The grey of dawn. First yawnings of reason...)

"—The 'real world'—an idea no longer of any use, not even a duty any longer—an idea grown useless, superfluous, *consequently* a refuted idea: let us abolish it!

"(Broad daylight;...all free spirits run riot.)

"— We have abolished the real world: what world is left? the apparent world perhaps?...But no! *With the real world we have also abolished the apparent world!*"

David
Gascoyne

Friedrich Nietzsche
(From: How the "Real World" at last Became a Myth,
in Twilight of the Idols.)

editor of *Velocities*, has published his poems in *Isaac Asimov's Science Fiction Magazine*, *Amazing Stories*, and the final issue of the British magazine *New Worlds*. Joron is coauthor with Robert Frazier of *A Measure of Calm* (Ocean View Books 1985), and author of a poetry collection *Force Fields* (Starmont House 1987). He has twice received the Rhysling Award for best science fiction poem of the year.

Andrew
Joron

Each step echoes
  in the interstices of this knowledge
  a passage lost
Miles underground
— entering the great hall
We see each page: a silvery lattice
Revolving in the dust

... a sudden flux of chronons
Signals *the Reading has begun*
Our monads of sense
  become tiny crustaceans
Flickering toward the unbounded machine

Each moment is sealed
& cross-referenced
  to the next creation

Each word has its own history
  spherical
Its center suffused with silence

Each sentence
  may be a volcanic island
Risen out of the bed of deep-sea darkness
Cooling as it remains
  bare of vegetation
  mirrored in its own lagoon

The caul's hung on a line

Andrew
Joron

While drying, its long stomata
Drone like parchment in the wind

These huts — each one, a heavy stone
Overgrown
With red gangrenous lichen
Dispirit the bowels
The mineral book whose leaves are layered
Deepest in the earth

Upon their roofs a radial foliage
Emits at light-speed
Steady messages of the dead

— & the roots of stars
Dangle down to tap that glistening speech

TWO WALKERS ACROSS THE TIME FLATS

Andrew
Joron

I.

How the trees
Stand here, like statements of loss
In some forgotten tongue

Lake also is a word that escapes us
— eyeless organisms
Move in its depths
Feeding on the rain of flesh

II.

When the sky fills up
We will notice, at all hours
A scarcity of light

& understand *distance*
As a plain populated by pillars of bone

I.

The town of Mandala is watched over   *Andrew*
By machine intelligence   *Joron*
— perhaps a satellite
Dimly descended to the Earth
Artifact from the time of tyrants
        it hangs there
        supplanter of the Sun
Its searchlights play across the crowd below
        a pulsing eyeball
— a mind weapon freed from orbit

& calls to mechanick brothers
Each poised above the other villages
        on this desert
        rerunning rituals
        it sings the song of SURVEILLANCE
Our breaths
Suspended in its radiance

For we are its perfected folk: made uniform
& genderless
— speaking only
In the language of our robot rulers
A series of darkly measured whispers
        we are as clouds
Converging on some abstract truth

II.

At the end of every avenue
In the circular city
there stares a monumental Eye of Power
        empinnacled
        on a whirlwind
Inaudibly it roars... subliminal commands
& blessings hourly

Andrew
Joron

The eye that devours
        light/ leaves the world
White & substanceless
        as the interiors of our words
A collection of doorways, cubes & columns
Evacuated of desire

While at the oases
Ancient trees are traumatized
& sink into the sand
Under the eye: grain molders in silos
The weather is changed into an ideogram
        that is not for us
        to understand

        III.
We march: our limbs turning
        ceremonious wheels

        though we move
Uncertainly, in long procession
        toward
That numinescent gaze
A steely mirror no larger than the Moon
        wherein our souls are melted
Multi-distanced
        & marked with stigmata
Forever lost in that blue alembic

Our bodies the living counters
Crushed on a concrete surface
        finely
        delineated as a gameboard

Creation
Becomes a dance
        like
Parthenogenic pinba

We stop & go
       according
       to a calculus of mental pressures
Harmony is pre-established

Under the eye: we advance
       a humming presages the final voice
The children are resealed in silken cusps
— unchosen ones are left to gambol
       in the drainage area
All futurity wears the head of an insect

       (the voice begins
To address the god)

Andrew
Joron

poems have appeared in *Under 30*, *Rocket Candy*, *New Worlds*, *Galaxy*, and *Velocities*. His own books of poetry are *Ironic Holidays* (Sariya Press 1965), *Les Papillon* (Lupo Press 1966), *Sludge Gulper 1* (The Basilisk Press 1971) and *Calibrations* (Allegany Mountain Press 1981). His poem "Limits" appeared in *Isaac Asimov's Science Fiction Magazine*, and is reprinted by permission.

Born in Berkeley, California and raised in Saudi Arabia, Lunde is a member of the Science Fiction Writers of America, and the Science Fiction Poetry Association. Formerly poetry editor of *Riverside Quarterly* and managing editor of *Drama & Theater*, he is now editor and publisher of The Basilisk Press, and contributing editor of *Escarpements Magazine*. He was awarded the Academy of American Poets Prize in 1967, and a Yaddo Colony fellowship in 1972.

David
Lunde

You'd have thought after Darwin
all this was obvious,
old news flapping in the park.
What did you say after all
but that there is no God,
no purpose to all this commotion,
that the intelligence of the atom
is as accidental as atmsophere?

But you should have known, Jacques,
the descendants of accident
would be the junkies of reason:
the seemingly endless recession
of waves from the universal shallows,
that effect of the magnetic moon
on the vanity of water,
has conveyed to each searcher
the answer he searched for.

And all true! The only answer
is my answer. It is there
that we start, that we did start,
we and the wiggling world
equally lightning and slime,
so that now with the sound in our ears
like a train in a sunken tunnel
of the universe washing away from us
for no reason that we know,
let us love one another
and instruct the idiot world.

David
Lunde

Like the microwave backflash
of the opening cosmos,
faint light suffuses Earth,
a directionless glow
exposing to clinical stars
the wind-scoured snowcrust
wrinkled with ash-dunes:
dumb tumuli humped
liked cursed barrows
on the bones of man's passions,
clinging to each encysted dream,
irradiating it like a cancer.

David
Lunde

Still the universal shrapnel hurtles
outward into emptiness,
defining Creation as itself,
while I rest on a rock
picking gravel out of my knees,
pondering quasars and the quantum jump.

The limits of knowledge
become increasingly apparent
weeding the garden. Undaunted
by the inorganic universe,
life flexes everywhere from earth,
splitting stone into soil
with algal patience, remaking
the world in its own image, and dying
into the mouths of its children.

When electrons vanish, to reappear
like spies in new circles
with new signatures, it is no more
marvelous to me and no less
than the sprouting of these seeds
in my care. And if quasars downshift
into red to demonstrate the distance
between observation and knowledge,
they show also that our frontier expands
as close to forever as we will ever need.

The planet turns, conserving
angular momentum, and this side of it
slips into shadow that allows
the universal light, omnipresent echo
to microwave hosannahs, to fall
on this square of orderly life.
The incomprehensible and familiar sky
opens before me
like a tract of uncleared land,
and if death is in fact God,
as it is worshipped, still
I will bruise my knees with gardening
but not with prayer.

David
Lunde

David
Lunde

At dusk when the life-sippers drink
here in the mosslands
and the high whine of their wings
accentuates the silent emergence
of stars, I stare back
through the warp of space and time
back to our collective beginning
back to the dim glow of Sol—
utterly invisible
save to nostalgic eyes—
attempting the transcendent act
of imagination necessary
to believe my alien blood
once fed some parasite of Earth.

of San Francisco, has been a MacDowell Colony Fellow, and on-the-air
poet at Pacifica Radio, KPFA Berkeley. His books of poems include *Her
Children Come Home, Too* (Sceptre 1972), *Damage Within the Com-
munity* (Panjandrum Press 1973 and 1977), *Chronicle* (Mother's Hen
1974), and most recently *The Singing Men My Father Gave Me* (Menard
1980). He has contributed to *Antigonish Review, Contact II, Frank, Pan-
jandrum, Velocities,* and many other magazines around the world.

Mycue began "Threshold to a Far Distance" in 1974; it soon took shape
as a sequence of ten poems under the title "Falling into Freedom." The
work continued to grow/expand/accrete. In 1977, Holmganger's Press
(Whitehorn, California) published it as a 30-page chapbook, *Root, Route,
& Range*, with cover by painter Richard Steger. The manuscript kept
growing, and in 1979, Papercastle Press (Melbourne, Australia) brought
out the 80-page *Root, Route, & Range: The Song Returns*. "Threshold
to a Far Distance" is now a poem-novel of three parts and 136 pages,
glimpsed here in an excerpt from its latest incarnation.

THRESHOLD TO A FAR DISTANCE
an excerpt

Edward
Mycue

13
Where the wind begins
turning the high-seated
boulders, ridges vibrate
luring footsteps
sprouting dreams
on uneven, blank brink —
bald flanks
of steep blue mountains —
tongues castellated with crags,
sheer falls —
and the lung-worm, lice
are meditations
of spectres rising
over this world.

15
In the icy mirror
genealogists discount
the framework,
but are not daunted
by ruins.
Ingenious
running
blood is buried
in grass
under the ice.

17
In this old journey
the declining sun
sets the sea on fire
before it sets.
On the shore —
a padlocked gate.
Under the marmalade waves —
a chain of accidents.
Creation myths are burning
in the spray —
between the two horizons,
out of the soil
the rose smoke
of stories
precipitates tears
into the seven main heavens
coursing from yesterday's prayers.

Edward
Mycue

20
Between average creeping
hill
and burning blacktop
lane
we've learned mysteries
of circus owner
and citizen clowns
how peace
units fall
of sheer rot
that berries mold
technologies
misfunction.

Edward
Mycue

30
Sloping
into the cradling
distance
fringed
with binding possibilities,
seeking the balance
eye
that has a crack
across it,
quiet windows, sighting
veins conceal
everything
pictured inside —
near-nature, house-
city, closet-
enthusiasm.

31
What
is retained
is a dream
of the sun.

Thick hands
stretch across
dead light,
and like flashfire
in chimney,
sapphire horizons
soar
into eyes
that reach back
into long-
fingered
grey fields,
pink-
drenched flesh
as the road
goes up/
over
the sky
line.

*Edward
Mycue*

Edward
Mycue

37

Blue drummings nuzzle closely
like a sack of rage
on a rotting wall of clapboards
hanging on a shed.
How close winter is —
hot sun knitted to chill air,
a barrier of briars,
wreaths of wasteland cross-woven
between wrongs, river
blades, bogs, mud, bottomland
a drizzle of masses.
A short wooden stake;
the first carved angel;
the whiter world a cavity
of graspable night shrinking
into stubby, crawling monsters
hell-browed — well-fleshed
with firm ascendency:
short-fingered sleep, twisted
visions.

39

When [if] a man starts out, as a traveler,
suddenly he becomes a hod carrier
and is then transformed into a lighthouse
crystallizing the blank in his mind
where the keynote of sincerity
is a mainspring drifting down the sands
of time living in the indolent dreaming
velvet gardens until he hears
an explosion going down the street
and he remembers he forgot his umbrella
or when a man starts out in the presence
of cats or a man starts out to flutes
and drums or starts out from a palace
of dung, he does start out and he meets
a menace and he may retreat, he may
run away, he may withdraw or not or
maybe he does not meet anything at all
but he is absorbed.

Edward
Mycue

53

Even in the valley
of death
life is buzzing
into a suffusing, soaring
sensation of light.
We continue pruning,
fertilizing, seeding
to bind and graft
a sash of lesions
to willowblush
and hummingbird.
In it molding, frothing
pallor
we let summer go — a
small brown box
of moth-eaten handles
and a fork of straw.

Edward
Mycue

63
What
has been
squandered
is
the
rain,
is
a
mire
of
stars
prospecting
union,
is
force
of
sound
fallen
shimmering.

74
Locked in a language
of clarity,
alone,
we cannot see or name
ourselves.
Slant blue light,
traditions
and gardens,
and an atlas of excavations
may reveal
nothing.

76
Shouting out
of a prism
of feeling,
the curtain rises
with the tenor mute.
One feels the bursting's
burst inside.
The cave's collapse
is prefaced
by the clock-maker,
the ascetic
voluptuary.

Edward
Mycue

84
An egg
is a splendid cage.
Sheep
ate the shepherd.
Failed
I feel safe
from Armageddon,
from the wolf of the magic town.
Who will light the new fire,
who will worship, dance,
can sow, and care, and gather?
Will I live through night——
night nacreous and still?
Memories again awake
to hear my call.
But it is dawn —
again, dawn
— dawn a time for death and travel.

Edward
Mycue

85

Memories reflect mirrors
from some outer rim
of brownrot, slaypest,
of uprooting the describable ash.
It's a stairway that strung
together and then stripped-away
until there is nothing but the stripping.
It is havoc shouting out of a prison
of feeling to flail cut flowers
in their newest clothes; to thresh-
out a void to flesh-out real loss.
It terrifically speaks throngs enough:
like Venetian magenta death, like
coming home to a destructible city.

With a free-fall
displacement
rooted
as the randomness of love, faintly
luminescent, translated
like radioactive wastes into particles
of menace
like spores of the destroying angel
in mutable transformations we are
states
of actions viewed in the process of
becoming through
relationships where everything
possible
affects behavior anytime, like fox-fire
in the rotten wood.
But these are other Springs.
Spring promises aren't certain.
There are still state lotteries
and taxes on salt;
harmonies do not resolve
dissonance to consonance;
but the certain, sharp, cold pitch
is indicated
as beach stones hiss away the waves
and the gardenia raves mad before extinction.

Edward
Mycue

Edward
Mycue

92
Sailing, sliding
past thrones, wolves, past priests
who pray for blood with loving lips,
like tramp stars that move
in smooth irregularity, the hanging key's
continual bending can bridge
disjunctured members.
Lizards and roses.
The fallen choir worms into the enchanted
casket, and all that is a lie confirms
the sacrament of bleeding.
Of bleeding. As bleeding. Two kids.
Two kids carrying one ladder adhere
to the break-up of what will be revealed,
imperfectly
apprehending creatureliness, begin
to see fire, trials in small things,
and memorizing the manner of doing deeds
here, as living stones shrink from the costs
of water, blood, or resurgent resurrection.

As sequined wheels, repeated glints,
lacinate through patterned days
like a sullen synchrony of impulses
deflecting in an orange mist
refracting in a hollow dawn—
within such all-enduring streams in time we move
through immediate lands
:into keys
:of over/out
:of up, down
shuttered [surface, psychic]
between realisms.
And as our motives brim-over
with secrets, regrets
to suggest dark's a great restorer
and light's a chalk block,
out of the earth
the consumed and folded past sprouts
mottled, brilliant, has binding possibilities,
a repeated beat, perpetually eluding
streets, faces, harbors, the unicorn's remains.
But each arcing sun still sets the concrete
on fire the way rose quartz glows
in pale though fractured vigor
writing lines that twist in ruins
of ridiculous survivals
like pollen dust
left behind with lights in the water.

Edward
Mycue

240

Edward
Mycue

107

After separation, time's
on the margin:
and as the train left Bruges
rows of poplars marched
along the lanes guarding, or guiding,
waterways in the fields.
Following the crimson logic
of what went before
scattering splinters of light
on familiar seas
repeated glints
of patterned days
flashed like lemon-emerald discs
strapped on a Ferris Wheel
while breath
in a luminous
penumbra
of hammer-cycles
of bumblebee and butterfly
failed upward
in a tilt
of sleep
toward a flute-
toned infinity of stress.

Like snowdrops in hedgerows,
the listening,
the wise young judge,
and fettled rhythm, these
are not dead: they sleep
mirrored in custom
set in space in time.
For if the stone is not lost
it halts into essential elements.
Then until some phoenix
stuns self-pity a waterfall
is an ornament
but moonlight is a gift
that changes
what it covers:
it is the weapon silence.

Edward
Mycue

Edward
Mycue

119
Here is an old journey,
millions of eyes, the stage
burst with people,
with unexpected mountains sloping
into the cradling distance.
In the occupied spaces
where light is a mystical text,
through the right ear of the moon
what are the connections
where anger, fear, and suffering
stand still in the iris?
It is the private gone public,
Joan of Arc perishing
in the surviving flames.
The red gladiola is her flower.
This is the garden of unfamiliar manners
where life is divided
in piles of colored dust,
and the infolding of the leaf
perpetually erodes the center of the circle,
where the twilight face of Plato
covers the mask of Mars. Here
horizontal realization is thrown up
vertically into localities
of timeless presence.

122

How could I jump for *you?*
I watch a tongue of blue flame,
a tongue castellated with crags, sheer
falls.
I am passing on
through the darkness, making haste
before the ear will be deaf,
making my way to the gardens.
Form is future's secret
feet move away with. *There*
between no beginning
and without an end
lyric spiralling and the leafing mesh
survive, like green shoots,
in a bowl of dust.
Here is my seat
though almond-blossom be riven.
I am my eye, and listen, drink,
melt old brain buckets
snowing ball, chain, structures;
carve, chisel, dance;
make prophets give way
to live without negative consciousness.
The road goes up/over the skyline.

Edward
Mycue

244

Edward
Mycue

123
Let us weep stars
when the night is clear
with contradictory clarities.
Nothing is forever.
Let us weep stars, ladders,
not blasphemies of light.
A sounding hierarchy
of airborne motive in the ear.
Sky is the *casa verde*, a trick factory
of winnowing spores,
bursting butterflies, dead figures
in the grass.
Over that green house, blind rains sweep
constant with chameleon expectations
draining colors of their smells,
leaving behind new stratas, locusts
ravening accumulated messages.
But inside, harmonizing
the frames of my own thoughts—
chromatic chosen apples
and brown desert squirrels—
not content with the old verse
dreaming out the seeds of time,
I am seeking the balanced eye.

Light
Light?—
Light   *Edward*
sounds: *Mycue*
useless,
struck with a stick.
Root,
Route,
and Range:
persist.
The drifting,
dawn, must settle,
but: it waits,
a bit,
until:
our very breathing
takes
identity . . . This is where
the song: begins.

has been Mission Planning Engineer for the Voyager II spacecraft project. He is a Fellow of the British Interplanetary Society, and is active in the American Institute of Aeronautics and Astronautics. On the literary side, Post has over 300 publications to his credit, and is a member of the Science Fiction Writers of America, Mystery Writers of America, and the Science Fiction Poetry Association. He is perhaps, the only person simultaneously listed in Jane's *Who's Who in Aviation and Aerospace* and *Who's Who in World Poetry*.

Jonathan
Post

We are all the stillborn child of Marie
We saw through her womb the blue Radium she
saw glowing through her Polish eyelids

Before we are born we are bumped, bicycles
for Mother and Pierre, master of crystals,
sweeping Radon from their lungs in sweet French air

Why should we die so young? Eve will be born
will learn piano, will hear her father's death
was instantaneous, head crushed, wheels spinning

Mother's strength will slip away, dressed all in black
she wrestles with radioactivity
wins prizes, loses the war with alpha rays

Irene will carry on the work, our parents
used to wonder: what color will Radium be?

It was a natural defense they had
these dinosaurs of our past life's regions
becoming invisible when asleep
assuming no invulnerability
of dreams, but transparency of breathing.

Faced by dangers in the dripping swamp
they would fade to the ground, insensible
insensate, the club-moss barely stirring
scaly visions nor ponderous perfumes.

Small toothy crawlers, caravans of fur
eased them into dormancy, with a taste
insidious as the bubbling asphalt pits
and would not let them wake. We find their bones
mineralized, in attitudes of rest.

Jonathan
Post

Jonathan
Post

Sometimes I forget why I came here. The City is so large, so noisy, so con-
sumed with pride and jammed with traffic. Stone towers rise ever higher
against the sky, and garbage rises ever higher in the streets. No one is safe
from thieves or bureaucrats. Rats chew human bones in the rubble at the
edge of town.

I cannot take it any longer. I will leave the city soon. I will save a little
money, then I will quit my job. Yes, and sail away to somewhere beautiful,
somewhere distant, maybe even home. These constant negotiations, the
rebellious workers, the tardy messengers, the substandard building materials
and broken tools and angles that are not true... Oh, I will sail away forever.

No, I am talking foolishness. It is all nothing. Tonight I will drink with you in
the tavern, which is not the fine place it used to be, and tomorrow I will go
to work again. Work, work, work, until this city subsumes the world. This
crazy town the native know as Babel.

> "And the Lord said 'Behold the people is one, and they have all one
> language; and this they began to do; and now nothing will be
> restrained from them, which they have imagined to do. Go to, let us
> go down and there confound their language, that they may not
> understand one another's speech.' So the Lord scattered them
> abroad from thence upon the face of all the Earth: and they left off to
> build the city. Therefore is the name of it called Babel."
>
> *Genesis 11*

Like leaves we scattered when the city died,
like frightened birds; I set my hammer free.
The potter left his wheel, the smith his fire;
shadows flowed like wine on all the roads.

The mortar dries half-mixed and mixed with rain;
green fills the fountains, and the walkways rot
in the summer sunlight drunk with flies.

Jonathan
Post

Sky sweeps the evergreens, the wind
spins in courtyards that the birds abandoned;
ruts left by carts explode with weeds
and weeds push open cracks between the flagstones.

The tower topples, one brick at a time,
one wall to a season. Babel's dust is washing to the sea.

Jonathan
Post

Enzyme Love, split me from the world
whose bond to me is solitude.

Free my blood of inhibition,
my brain's accumulated walls

of constant regulation,
over-concentrated will.

Consume in airless darkness
concerts of sour dreams.

I burn for this conversion.
Lead me to the pathway.

Transport me from environment,
from cellular compartment

to the open system, energy,
the cycle I was born to.

self-styled Scientist of the Strange, enjoys an international reputation as poet, novelist, playwright. His dramas for British television include *Leap in the Dark, Jack Be Nimble,* and *Miss Carstairs Dressed for Blooding.* His eight radio plays have won major awards including the Prix Italia (1982). Among his novels-of-the-fantastic are *In the Country of the Skin* (1973), *The God of Glass* (1979) and *The Sleep of the Great Hypnotist* (1979), all under the Routledge & Kegan Paul imprint. He also is co-author, with Penelope Shuttle, of *The Wise Wound,* a psychological study of the human fertility cycle.

Redgrove's poems have been published in the Penguin *Modern Poets* series, *The Oxford Book of Twentieth Century Verse,* and in *Manhattan Review, Antaeus, The Atlantic Monthly, New Worlds,* and elsewhere. His fifteen major volumes of poetry published since 1960 have won innumerable awards. He reads often on forays from his home in Cornwall and has recorded two LPs of poetry for Argo Records. The poems collected in *POLY* are new to print.

THE POWER

Peter
Redgrove

The root which is called a drug
That converses about all the doings of roots,
About the brilliant candle of its tip,

Flame-tip in a world lighted by millions of such candles,
To the visible eye as black as the black earth
Adam brought out of Paradise, blacker than black.

It is the broken bridge, the black
Pontefract, the black daemonic host;
Or the black spider, ordering her web,

Like the nuclear reactor at the centre of the grid,
And the cobweb which is a silken balcony,
The mannequins and models caught in her big store,

In the glassy threads which are streets of windows.
And the woman purchasing her secret laboratory
of distillations, along the criss-crossing routes,

The woman in her threads, her shining spoors.
Out of the black centre of our experience
She enters, a sudden arrival of living detail

Of bold-smashed outlines, disruptive colours,
And the bolder undiscerned colours she distils,
For she works the whole air with her power through her sleeves.

Every sound-wave travelling to your ear   *Peter*
Bears with it at its Godspeed a delicate   *Redgrove*
And rhythmical heat-process,
Giving up its small warmths with each word.
The breath rattles in his lungs
Like stones in a brook. There is a ship announced,
It is his death-ship, he believes,
And named *Midnight Court*. Can it be
This platform approaching through the warm night
Like a great skating-rink on the water
Lighted white with its small figures moving
In bright colours about its hawsers? Above it
There is a cloud that opens infinitely at the top,
A visionary cloud that brightens
What it surrounds, like the scents
That cluster like a necklace
About her adored throat. His bed
Is in the library, and there is light
Printed on every page, and outside
In the warm mist that is clearing, looms of light
Dripping with dew, dew on the grass
Like the bright print reflected up,
Passing over the library ceiling as you turn the pages.
Now it is a table with a closed sleep on it,
And he has shut his book, and is reading it,
The handsome leather, sleeping; a book about
The lightning-that-sees, a branching chain
Of what we call dead people holding hands,
Not blinking, not speaking, showing.
We pass our lives
Close to those folding fire-doors, and every sound
You speak carries with it through the air
Its delicate heat-process in warm scent and rhythm.

Peter
Redgrove

An insect resembles horses, with jalousies
For coolness, don't we prefer
The hot-blooded, the silken-nosed,
The hempen-maned, since
The insect glistens so, voids
Crystalline excrement, invisibly breathes.
Where are the clouds of hay-scented racing-breath,
Soft gallops across green banquet? Can one prefer
Snowfields before brooks, crystal-sets
To warm mediums in sweating trance?
Ah, but the insect comes like rock crystal
With its purpose exactly set through aeons,
It is the executive of vegetation, reader
Of messages in a chemistry on the barks,
Bud, leafskin, petal, and that bee
Is flying stamens, this butterfly
A posy-postman made of flowers, inspect
That beetle and consider the winged acorn
Of forests, and in the fly's beard,
In its hairy lip, the wheatfields blow.
Watch a horse, see a warm creature,
An independence on four hooves; but the insect
Is a crystal of that green creature everywhere
That walks in wings and leaves and winds, each journey
On spindle legs and droplet body fits every other,
Green steed of wheatfields and lianas and all the oceans;
See, that butterfly flutters with its tides,
That hive hums with its breezes; under the boughs
Our confused horses rush hot-bloodedly.

The sealed book of his heart   *Peter*
Full of scrolls of oxygen   *Redgrove*
Bursts its lockets
And the locket at his neck bursts
The tall vein there ripped off like a tie
His collar exploding,
The grenade of his heart,
And in the sudden heat and light
The lungs open wide their gates
With a great shout *Zohar*!

His whole vocabulary
All the words he has spoken, whispered, sung
In one shout
That is stout
Like a dictionary snatched
Out of the fire and flung
Over the abyss flaming,
A star shattering into words of every hue

The electrical bine
Piped in vertebral thorns
Shook and slowly reddened,
St. Elmo's fire at every fingerprint,
A corona of slow-motion burning
Like a Christmas pudding of illuminated brandy
Carried in in its holly crown
With its sweet smell of blood and fruit
Full of silver money
Slack bag of money and pudding slowly
Slumping to the spittle floor
Among the tobacco embers
The teeth gnawing aslant in the head
Like a pudding eating itself

Peter
Redgrove

And the too-many birds of his soul
In the threshing of his blood tree
The birds which should be one bird
Beating its wings steadily in his heart
Fluttered everywhere
Catching St. Elmo's fire
And flew with greater wings of flame
In oiled colours up his chimney
And the carrions of him sparkled like soot upflying
Buzzing sparks of the hearth

All the spirits flew up and sideways

And the soul fell back
And dove into sappy rock
Rejoining the water it was made of
And lay in strata
Like wardrobes
Like crisp shirts
Slowly purified in the laundries of geology and pressed
Slowly slowly into new ghost
Rising in vents fumaroles and drains
Just a hint of him here
To his friends in that gutter
In the babbling of that gutter-voice
Or returning from its carousals in the sky
Like rain, and not like a ghost

And in cold winter
Lying like crisp shirts ready to be worn again
Surprised and finding themselves
So clean and sparkling with such cool colours
And with such silence after that fat brief bloody shout.

I.

In front of slaves' eyes in the markets   *Peter*
they rotated a potter's wheel to check   *Redgrove*
Whether they were liable to fits.

II.

Infrasonic sounds of storms at sea
Generate in coastal towns mass seasickness,
Rocking on great bass waves you cannot hear.

III.

A charge caught on an insulator
Such as the highly-charged electrostatic
Field carried by the lacquered hair
Of a passer-by, sexy, no? Not entirely;
The handclasp crackles, the lightning-bolt
From a kiss chips a tooth.

IV.

To compound this she wears
A nylon raincoat that
Generates further charge by rubbing folds.
And wires she passes pick up currents from her moving field,
She generates life in any conductor, induces fields
In any non-conductor, the minx.

Peter
Redgrove

V.

Doorbells ring out as she passes down the street
Which lightens with flung-open doors
As puzzled householders run to check the engines
Of their parked cars that rev up and sound
Their warning instrument choking to silence as she walks
Out of the metal's ken, and there is
An appalling static blocking all police-calls,
A white noise on all the black telephones.

VI.

Yet we celebrate our electricity together.
I lift the sparkling champagne-glass
That rings and echoes to its small round storms
And toast your crackling long blue skirt I swear
Is compounded of rain and lightning, and is
This diamanté watch I fasten round your wrist not full
Of tiny branching stars at all the tips
Of cogs meshing in the dark? We hold hands,
they crackle like cellophane or tuning foreign stations
Because above, around, the stars join radiant grips.

The electrical fire is easily obtained
by the working of glass;
It is the quick air when caught.
The burning of shells too gives
Quick air, for the powdered shell
Has it in its phosphorescence,
And the sea-lantern purveys it
Glowing upon the waters,
The Nautilus; and the fish
Offer themselves quick to the night seabirds
For they glow up to them from shallows.
What of the stately
Night-exploding bird of sunset
That is red because it is heightened darkness,
Or of dawn that is the passionate blue
Of darkness lightening, when on this sea
Every wave is as a chord of the whole water
Fretting through its world-straits in shadows
Of reflected waves or seiches? There is
On the one hand the full soprano pond,
And at my left the carrick Roads with a seiche rate
Of ringing back its shadows of thirty minutes;
Does this water not see the light as it feels the land
Pressing the air in seiches, the whole air
That rings like a bell
With the clapper of earth? What is
Your seiche rate as we rock together
To and fro in our waves, and the action
Sends back its shadow-crests; as the bell
Shines itself by ringing so the metal skirt
Fills to the hem with music, bass waves
Rolling over the sunny water, quick air.
Now the astronaut approaches in his foil suit
Shining in remembrance of the spirit world,
For putting two bodies in their quick together
Recreates their spiritual form
In quicklight by which we see the moon,
A long place full of children,
A long white lane used as a playground.

Peter
Redgrove

Peter
Redgrove

The ocean of air carried on the shoulders;
We are pressed a little flat, like deepsea fishes,
So let us ride on the windroads,
Then our organs will round out
And our eyes will not need glasses;
They have travelled sufficiently now
To have seen spirits, to be capable:
At twenty miles high, nacreous clouds
With the sheen of innermost shells;
At fifty, those noctilucents hanging
Big as cities that are always shining
Being exalted enough to see the sun always;
At seventy, auroras of electricity
Like visions preceding sleep; the superhuman
In everything.

The every-turning wheel of the weather,
the cloud-shadows flitting over the grass like ironed ghosts;
How a shock-echo of thunder can start the whole sky spinning;
Smell thunder everywhere!

The spirit-light of past time in the candle.
Watch its shadow of forests flickering on the ceiling,
It is a wax recording, the prehistoric excrement
Of trees, laundered by the ages, playing. Ignite
The slow dynamite and inherent light
Streams out, with its swashing shadows;
Sunlight streams out of the oiled soil, the past
Packed with its lamps, blazing from candles.

The spirits shed bones like white hairpins

As they ascend, loosening themselves from time
Like brilliant shadows igniting as they ascend
To someplace they can always find the sun,

Peter
Redgrove

Turning at the door ajar for a blessing of rain
Becoming cloudscapes that are cascades of water-crystals
Transmitting a continuous radio as they rise;
But the Lord calls me down, from the wet.
I see the fat wet girls running
For shelter in the smell of thunder everywhere
And I rejoice in its sound that keeps the whole world wheeling;
And the wet cyclists with the open necks,
Lightning glitters in their wheels
And as they dash through puddles with their two round wings
They pronounce the great echoes inherent in their machines
Of pigeons breaking cover from the storm-wet woods.

I.

Peter
Redgrove

The grey sculptor in his dusty studio,
The stone-butcher, Slater.

The shut snail of coiled slate
Hanging by its foot to the limestone pillar
Of the once-barn,

Having scooped its curly self-stone
Out of salad of weeds and water,
The stone scroll it inhabits,

Reading absorbed by snail-light this text from the inside.

II.

The cold sunshiny universe.
Woven mats of sunlight slipping over the choppy sea.
Vaults of sunshine created in the water,
Deep crypts arched into the pleated water,
The water salt with stone licked off the land with its foot
Turning its pages over and over by sea-light,
Its roomy dripping pages full of milt and mackerel.

III.

The bone knitting-needles plot the baby's covering,
The woven coverlet, as inwardly she
Knits the baby together, cobbles
The skin of doe of her daughter,
The slender pins and bone-tacks of the hand,
The haberdashery and software of the being,
The materiel it inhabits, the pomp to which
The great couturiers are shadowy fashion,
The cobbler's womb-shop, the lower place,
The leathery cellar, brightly lit.

IV.

The studio of the blood with its golden windows
Where the sculptress is working without pause,
Long before dawn, working hungrily,
Working hungrily as she breakfasts.

Peter
Redgrove

V.

The tree has cast its net like a conjuration.
In the air of shadows last night I swear
The net was empty; this morning
It has caught a miraculous draught of pink blossom.

VI.

The mirror waiting to slip on her reflection
Like a cool silk
As the womb was ready to slip on its reflection;
The magic glance of a woman
Who will not lie with the child inside her,
The secret sharer.

VII.

The snail that peruses its inner life and
The milk-bottle full of silk in the sculptor's studio.
The sculptor remakes the outer world, with his slaty pencil,
The sculptress remakes the inner, in bright light.
The silky bottle, one of Slater's models for the inner:
A pearl-piercing spider crouched in a shirt of pearls,
Its white-bearded face peers out of the circular collar.

VIII.

He dreams of troops countermarching on a green field;
The snail dreams cloudy saps crystallising into language;
She dreams of a person both invisible and visible at once;
The spider (if that is what it is)
Dreams pearls patterning within pearls pearl upon pearl.

writes: "Although I already spoke English, French and Spanish as a child, my education, up to the age of sixteen, was almost exclusively in the Classics, in Latin and ancient Greek, so that I was more familiar with Euripides than with Shakespeare and with Virgil than with Milton or Wordsworth. When I was only seventeen, some of my first English poems were nevertheless accepted for publication in *transition*, to which James Joyce and Gertrude Stein, among others, contributed regularly. These poems of mine were published there when I was barely eighteen and were soon followed by a few of my earliest prose poems, which were more visionary and lyrical than those that I know write, in fact more concerned with the aesthetics of the Sublime, than with those of the Absurd.

When I was twenty-three, *Poetry: a Magazine of Verse* then published me for the first time, so that I may now be its oldest contributor; a year later, T.S. Eliot published a group of my poems in *The Criterion*.

In spite of these encouraging beginnings, financial problems and deep concern over the rise of Fascism as well as health problems reduced me, from 1934 to 1945, to a serious depression in the course of which I underwent psychoanalysis with several different therapists. But these were also profoundly formative years, partly because I was then living in America for the first time, beginning in 1937, partly too thanks to my friendship with Paul Goodman in Chicago and New York as well as to my psychoanalysis. In 1946, I published with New Directions a critical work on the writings of Oscar Wilde and, a year later, my *Poems 1928–1948*. Pressure of work as a multilingual international conference interpreter then prevented me, for close to ten years, from writing or publishing much except in periodicals. After 1958, I gradually found more leisure for writing. *Dialogues on Art*, a volume of interviews of twelve living painters or sculptors, was thus published in London and New York as well as in a German translation in Frankfurt-am-Main. Twenty years later, it was reprinted as a paperback in Santa Barbara by Ross Erikson Publishers, who also published its sequel, *More Dialogues on Art*, a collection of interviews with twelve other painters.

Dialogues on Art was followed by a couple of books that I wrote and published in French, in Paris, later by *Magellan of the Pacific*, a biography of the great Portuguese navigator, which was published in London and New York as well as in an Italian and Portuguese translation. Black Sparrow Press then began to publish in Santa Barbara my collected poems, of which two volumes, *Emperor of Midnight* and *Thrice Chosen*, have already been published while the third, *A Private Life*, still awaits publication. At the present time I'm working on my memoirs.

In 1982, I was granted, by the American Academy and Institute of Arts and Letters, its annual Margery Peabody Waite Award "for constant effort and integrity in his art." On a number of occasions, I have taught, as a guest, at San Francisco State University, Brown University, The University of California at Santa Cruz, Oberlin College, and State University of New York at Binghamton, and I have been a contributing editor of VIEW (New York), *Antaeus* (New York), *Conjunctions* (New York), *L'Ingenu* (Paris) and one of the three editors of *Das Lot* (West Berlin). I have also published a number of books translated from French, Dutch, German or Turkish as well as, in periodicals, a great number of poems translated from these and a few other languages. In 1985, I thus published with Cadmus Editions, in California, *The Wandering Fool*, a volume of twenty translations, together with commentary, of poems of the thirteenth-century Turkish Sufi Dervish Yunus Emre; also, in Paris, a French translation of Horace Walpole's *Hieroglyphic Tales*, the earliest know example of automatic writing as it was practiced over a hundred years later by the French Surrealists.

I was born in Europe of American parents. In spite of my now having spent most of my life, for professional and other reasons, in Europe, and of my having also written and published a great deal in French, I have always considered myself primarily an American writer. My model for the prose poems now published here, has thus been Ambrose Bierce, whose *Parenticides Club* likewise served me as a model for my collection of fables or midrashic prose poems, *New Old and New Testaments*, that Red Ozier Press published a few years ago in a limited edition in New York.

Some of my writings have nevertheless been written in French or in German, others too have been published only in German, Italian, Portuguese or turkish translations. In recent years, I appear to have been slowly gaining a reputation of sorts also as a very marginal and eccentric advance-guard French writer. As such, I'm variously reputed in Paris to be of Rumanian, Egyptian or Turkish origin rather than an American.

All but my most recent literary archives are already preserved in the Special Collections Department of the Research Library of the University of California at Los Angeles. I have been assured that they are full of surprises, and that a thorough study of them would require familiarity with a good ten languages, including Arabic and Turkish.

Edouard
Roditi

Edouard
Roditi

The day that all watches and clocks suddenly stopped, we were reduced very much to our own devices to avoid ever being late, though even trains and planes, of course, could no longer keep to any predictable schedule. I've always been a dawdler, with a tendency to waste too much precious time, in fact to be a spendthrift too insofar as time is also money. But I'm fortunate in that I happen to be married to a wonderful housewife who, by dint of judicious economies, generally manages to make up for most of my losses of money and waste of time.

Anyhow, to put it briefly and thus avoid wasting any of your time too with unnecessarily detailed descriptions of our household and our daily life, my wife began to save time by bottling any spare time that we had not yet used and then storing it in the refrigerator. Whenever we needed to know the number of minutes required to boil an egg or to bake a cake, she would then pour the right amount of fresh bottled time into a glass or bowl and let it evaporate in the sunlight. Of course, we still had our difficult and timeless days, when the sky was overcast and a glass or bowl of time took longer to evaporate, so that an egg, instead of being soft-boiled, came out hard-boiled, or a potroast came out of the oven charred. You can always use a hard-boiled egg in a salad, and our cat even developed a taste for charred meat, so that we saved on canned cat-food on such days. Anyhow, we managed things much better than our neighbors, thanks to my wife's ingenuity, though I myself have never yet been able to acquire her proficiency in pouring, for instance, exactly ten minutes of fresh but invisible time into a glass. The trouble is that I don't seem to see time, even if I wear my reading glasses, as clearly as she does, so that one day I allowed the glass to overflow and thus wasted a good half-hour of precious time, though without seeing it, on the kitchen floor.

You should have heard my poor wife bawl me out when she came home from her bridge-party and had to mop up the mess, especially as wasted time very soon begins to turn sour and to form a greasy and fetid paste. That is why you should always bottle only the very freshest spare time.

Deprived of both weather and politics in a less stormy and more peaceful world, we no longer had any subject for tentative conversations as an opening gambit whenever we chanced to meet an utter stranger. You'll agree that you can't decently approach a newcomer by asking him point blank about the state of his finances, the pecularities of his sex-life or the quality of his daily stools. So we were all left practically speechless or reduced to discussing eternally the same few stale subjects in small groups of family and close friends.

After a while, however, some of us were fortunate enough to discover the charms of botany. Groups of local residents were soon organized to go out on expeditions in the surrounding countryside, where unusual leaves, grasses, flowers or weeds were culled and then compared and identified in excited and very competitive arguments, often with people one had never yet chanced to meet and who were sometimes as mysterious and odd as the botanical specimens that they proudly displayed. Violent quarrels even occurred, over a few such discoveries, when fraud was suspected, such as a leaf that might have been artificially bleached or stained. One joker even turned up one Saturday with an obviously home-made mandrake-root.

Botany led us in turn to develop an interest in the insect world, which kept us for a while very busy, if only with the more common varieties of lepidoptera. Later, we nevertheless found ourselves beginning to form hostile factions or political parties: those in favor of exterminating quite ruthlessly some species of arthropods that they deemed harmful, and those others who were just as determined to protect even the common flea and the bedbug as species that were already threatened with imminent extinction.

It thus turned out that it still takes all kinds to make a world, even fleas, bedbugs, political parties and experts ready to risk their credibility by predicting the results of the next local elections or tomorrow's weather, now that the weather had returned, together with politics, to bless us with its uncertainties.

Edouard
Roditi

Edouard
Roditi

I share my bed with nobody and everybody, with nothing and everything. When I retire there for the night, I see, of course, that I'm alone, but my privacy begins to be invaded as soon as I fall asleep. All sorts of people, many of whom I would be hard put to name or even to recognize at all, then see fit to go to great lengths to arouse my desires. Even animals, some of them of no recognizable species, often join in the fun and games, if such they can still be called. Objects too begin to assail me: I've been sodomized by the spout of a kettle, masturbated by a meatgrinder and been the recalcitrant husband of the mouth of a trumpet.

Among my nocturnal visitors, I have few favorites, but these are generally too discreet to appear frequently, nor do I know of any reliable means for summoning them at my will, so that I remain a victim of chance encounters that horrify me more often than they delight me.

If I wake up at night, I find myself, to my surprise, alone in bed. All these visitors vanish as mysteriously and as suddenly as they appear, so that I'm left wondering whether they really exist. Still, they *must* exist, or is it I who am a dream, in fact the one dream that they all have in common? Then why would they all have chosen to dream only of me, or do they also visit others whose sleep they haunt as they haunt mine? Do I share them and, if I do, with whom?

Until now, I always believed that they were my secret, my shame rather than my pride. Suddenly, I now begin to suspect that I may long have been sharing this secret with many others, each one of whom has been erroneously believing and may still believe, as I did too, that only he is haunted by all those nocturnal visitors. Perhaps, however numerous and varied they may seem to me to be, they are only one creature, but one that changes constantly its nature and appearance, or that adopts countless disguises to conceal from me its true being.

Perhaps too, nothing is real, not even I.

"An illogical language would be one in which, e.g., you could put an event into a hole."

Edouard
Roditi

Ludwig Wittgenstein: Notes dictated to
G.E. Moore in Norway, April 1914.

"Take it and bury it and see if it grows lilies."

Mae West, in Diamond Lil.

On the television screen we witnessed last night the funeral of the whole past. All of pre-history and of recorded history, beginning with the first chapter of *Genesis* and ending with our last Presidential Elections, was being discarded as obsolete or superfluous trash, thrown into a huge open grave, to be forgotten for all times and never to be rediscovered by any inquisitive archaeologists of a later age. From now on, come what may, we are all expected to believe that we are living in the Millennium, in the best of all possible worlds and an everlasting present that dawned on us without precedents or past and without any need of a more felicitous future.

Many of us, as we watched this program and listened to the funereal music which accompanied the ceremony in our national capital, felt a secret and poignant nostalgia for the innocence of their own personal childhood that was henceforth doomed to be no longer remembered, not even in dreams. As whole centuries passed rapidly before our eyes and vanished into the dark and bottomless pit, others also felt briefly that they might have lived more happily in another age, perhaps as Neanderthal men, in Imperial Rome or in Queen Victoria's Indian Raj at the time of her glorious Durbar. Whole civilizations, however, vanished in a twinkling before our dazzled eyes. Wars and massacres too were wiped out, as if they had never occurred.

Are we really destined to be happier now that we have been purged of our whole past, of all our feelings of guilt and our nostalgias too? I fear that many of us may still be tempted to haunt in secret the concealed site of the mass grave where so many memories of which we were once proud or ashamed are irretrievably buried. A few disloyal or ghoulish citizens are already predicting in a cautious whispering campaign that the earth which covers our forbidden past may soon bring forth some very strange crops.

Edouard
Roditi

I'm reading a book, alone in the living room of what use to be the country home of my parents in France, over fifty years ago, when I hear the phone ringing in the next room and hasten to answer it. But the next room turns out to be a quite unfamiliar kind of office. The call is for my mother, and the caller is an American friend of hers whom she first met in New York, many years after the sale of this country home, and with whom I myself have quarreled, long after my mother's death.

At first, when she recognizes my voice, this woman seems to be rather embarrassed, but soon begins to chat with me as if we had never quarreled. After a long conversation in the course of which she gives me news of a writer who is one of her closest friends but whom I avoid seeing since our quarrel, she asks me again if she can speak to my mother, who has arrived here only on the previous day but had written her from abroad, asking her to contact her here.

I begin to look for my mother throughout this huge house that is composed of countless rooms, some of them quite familiar, others unfamiliar, so that the house is like a mosaic of rooms from all the homes where I have ever lived, but with many too like those of hotels. At last, I find my mother fast asleep in a huge double bed in a darkened bedroom where the curtains are drawn. I decide not to awaken her and find my way back with great difficulty to the phone, to explain to her friend that my mother arrived here very tired after her long trip and is still sleeping. This woman then explains to me that my mother is dead and that she too is dead. I hang the receiver up and return to the living room, where I see on a table a great deal of mail addressed to my mother and begin to wonder where I should now forward it, since the dead leave no forwarding address.

When someone insulted me by calling me a worm, I tried hard for a while to imagine what my life might be if I really were a worm. But the trouble is that no worm, as far as I was able to gather, has ever felt offended by being called a man by another worm, so that all my attempts to understand a worm's feelings and life were doomed to frustration, for lack of any similar communication reaching me from the world of worms. It's much easier to imagine being a dog, even if you're not gifted with a tail to wag when you feel happy. How does a worm display its feelings, whether of pleasure or displeasure? It can't whine or bark, and its whole body is a kind of tail that wriggles but can't really be wagged. Is there a Heaven awaiting pious and saintly worms, and a Hell for those that are sinners? Can a worm be class-conscious or experience guilt-feelings? Do worms elect their President, or are they ruled by a Monarch? I shudder to think what they eat as they worm their way through the loam of my vegetable patch, and their sex life leaves me really perplexed.

So many questions about the life of worms remained unanswered that I soon had to give up imagining that I really was a worm. Now I content myself, for better or for worse, with sometimes imagining that I'm a dog, in fact my own pampered household pet. When I feel good, I reward myself with a chocolate cookie.

Edouard
Roditi

Edouard
Roditi

I live in a house that is always growing or shrinking. It sometimes has a hundred huge rooms or even more, but then can also become a small one-room shack. I often forget something, a book I've been reading or my wallet full of money, in one of its many rooms that I can never find again if I go back to seek what I've mislaid. But everything that I've lost turns up again, though in a new room that I can't remember ever having seen. A long time ago, I was still confused by having to live in such a home, but one becomes accustomed, in the long run, to anything and everything. Now nothing on earth can convince me that I might be happier elsewhere.

longtime editor of *Aldebaran Review*, is the executive director of Califor-
nia Poets in the Schools, and divides his year between Berkeley and Mex-
ico. A winner of the Anne Award for Poetry (1982), Simon's poems have
appeared in *Abraxas*, *Chelsea*, *Velocities*, *Poetry Northwest*, *Prarie
Schooner*, etc. His translations from Spanish can be found in the Com-
municating Vessels section of *POLY*.

The quality Gary Snyder described as John Oliver Simon's "surefooted-
ness" can be found in his dozen books of poetry: *Roads to Dawn Lake*
(Oyez 1968), *Adventures of the Floating Rabbi* (Runcible Spoon 1968),
Cat Pome (Gunrunner Press 1969), *Dancing Bear* (Undermine Press
1969), *The Woodchuck who Lives on Top of Mount Ritter* (Aldebaran
Review 1970), *A Ten Days' Journey From Badwater to Lone Pine*
(Aldebaran Review 1971), *Animal* (Aldebaran Review 1974), *Living in
the Boneyard* (Cat's Pajama's Press 1976), *The Panamine City Badman
Ballad* (Aldebaran Review 1976), *Rattlesnake Grass* (Hanging Loose
Press 1978), *Neither of us can Break the Other's Hold* (Shameless Hussy
Press 1981), *Shaved at Dawn* (Neon Sun 1984).

John Oliver
Simon

Living in the eternal digit of the present moment
I walked out the ancient causeway of Ixtapalapa
where mechanics chew their mid-day tacos with oil-black fingers
looking for a locality where rumor has it
they stretched the lucky victim on the broken throne
and kissed his heart and lit a cigarette inside his flesh.
The city wavers in the haze of the imperfect tense.
Yesterday we cut a pine tree down in the shadow
of Popocatepetl, and in the stone hearth of your ancient town
plugged in the rows of lights, small suns for Santa Claus
to find his way to Xochimilco. From that midnight orgasm
every new fire in the human world was kindled.

Time has a desire to circle round a point.
We picture ourselves pierced by its infinite arrows.
I walked up the barrio's dirt streets (some years
removed from the primal poverty of the lost cities).
A man with one eye in flames nodded hello.
I was turning you over and over in my mind
in one language or another. I was the oldest visitor
who ever signed the book in the little museum
and the only one from the other side of the river,
the only one who didn't live in Ixtapalapa.

Arrows, metates, clay faces. Your face, Senora,
woman who comes in my dreams as someone else,
conflicted, uncertain, half an hour late, leaving me
at the Metro, living in another sense of time
where it's hard to identify when an action begins,
hard to know when something's over. Today I know
the sun's as south as it ever gets in the Valley of Mexico.

Turning and turning you behind my eyes. What shall I do?
In a screen of memory I call last night we kissed
in your parking lot wondering while Orion rose
from behind the apartments of the Southern Forest,
a tall god of this galactic arm. Your fingers know
what to do with elements. Atoms of hydrogen
are simpler than the human heart, that sweet thorned fruit.

John Oliver
Simon

I walked through eucalyptus woods like Tilden Park,
wandered up steepening game paths of black scree
with many pre-hispanic artifacts of plastic,
passed a downward swarm of teenage boys in the glory
of their glands, chose a crevice above the road,
climbed panting. From here the smog cuts all
distances down. Dandelions grow out of the sacred
dark steps. This is the known place of beginnings.

And everywhere in the world they saw the fire
as if it were a new star. And they rejoiced exceedingly
because things could begin again, because the world
was new, like seeds, like babies, because the universe
wasn't going to spin to a stop in the dark and cold
of entropy, because there was enough mass to close space.
Similarly my father's people made a tree of lights
to remember their war of liberation. Out in that haze
somewhere you count the thin useless pesos out
for your Christmas shopping wondering about this
gringo suddenly in your life. Out in that haze
a few days or moments ago a spark erupted into a fireball
that ate a lost city. Silver factories, roar
of the ring road, intricate traffic of ants
on the ancient causeway of Ixtapalapa, a model
of the world of the distant past, in a museum.

John Oliver
Simon

I am your mystery and you are mine. If I had written this
in your language I could read it to you but as it is
I left my dictionary in the old hotel. And I may
have to climb, in the sunjunctive mood, contrary to fact,
through a high window with a broken screen
face downward in the dark void like a drunk thief,
like a tightrope walker on the strung wire of time
to find my keys and let myself in or out. Bells ring down
in the smog like hammers on old metal. I think
maybe I'll light a cigarette, a match glares
in the history of things, it only happens once,
I smoke a fire for another cycle, it measurably
shortens my life, I pretend it's your mouth
emptying smoke, pretend it's your tongue my tongue
touches in my empty mouth, in one language or another.

The good traveller doesn't know where he's going; the perfect traveller
doesn't know where he's been.

John Oliver
Simon

—an inscription in the guest book in Cafe Oscar's,
Arab sector of Jerusalem, February 1967.

There were times in the long journey
when you were not the perfect traveller.
The poem always asked you to travel toward it
and through it, allowing certain luminous moments
to become your carapace, the words
you licked into shape until they hardened around you.
The horizon modulating until it became a city
that a few years later or a thousand years before
was famous in the newspapers for bloodshed.
Peace surrounded you in your long journey
although sometimes the balloon was tenuous.
Dust rose from the lonely wheels
of the cheap bus, rain stained the bathroom walls
of the cheap hotel, and the poem sat all night
waiting by your pillow as you imagined
a perfect lover who had her own road
to travel, her own set of footprints
yet to be made, leading in another direction
across the dusty town, through the railroad station,
over bodies of water yet to be named
past the children's eyes collecting light
crying brilliantly in their own language.

MALINALCO

John Oliver
Simon

When Alberto and the poets came up here
eating God's flesh, hoping for mysterious
significance, playing at the rituals
of Don Juan and Castaneda, lightning
and thunder vomited from a clear sky
and they fell to their knees
begging the powers above and below to save them
happy at last to be alive
in the ordinary village below
with cigarettes and beer,
the whole world still throbbing
grimy rainbows through the rain.

I came up here uncertainly
willing that my words be awkward,
as if my native tongue
were a foreign language.

Today is Saturday.
I am feeling fine.
I am glad.
I am in love.
Would you be so kind as to bring me the bill, please.

In the den where the eagles and jaguars
are carved from the flesh of the living stone
the clock has not been reset since the Pleistocene.
This is the cave of God's sister,
the lady of grass,
the woman who puts languages
in the mouth of the stranger.

Teenagers in dark glasses from the world's navel,
that receptacle of megalopolis
long over-filled with human flesh and smoke,
carry a ghetto blaster among the ruins.
Danger! cries the oracle of heavy metal
in a foreign tongue that only I
can understand. Danger straight ahead!

Playing at a ritual
I spill water on the flesh of the living stone
in each direction, wishing to ask
permission to love
a woman of this country.

In the ancient convent down in the village
the world's a painted labyrinth of gardens
for the meditation of virgins,
with the bearded face of a god
in agony or orgasm
in the center of the burning rose.
Painted pillars support a real stone roof
and a false blue sky
stretches all the way to infinity
in the winged land of prayers.

God's sister could never be confused
with a virgin. When I slept with her
I came out covered with blood.
Her brother was a hummingbird in the mountain.
Her name was the same as my own.
It was common as grass.
She laid down with the snake,
she slept with the man with fangs
she gobbled up human hearts
they left for her on the polished feathers,
on the smooth fur of the living stone.

John Oliver
Simon

John Oliver
Simon

I hold my heart in my hands
calling aloud for love
as the slow
pulse we call time
throbs in my throat.
Already the blood is dry on the stone.
Roosters and mariachis resound from the village.
Children from the world's navel
test their balance on narrow
ledges laughing over a bone-
cracking void. The sky
is finally almost clear blue. I speak
a foreign language as if it were my own.

Today is Saturday.
The world is perfectly ordinary.
I am glad to be alive.
There are hidden powers.
I beg them for this love.
Bring me the bill!

Up canyon, past the green wooden crosses
that mark places of power,
in a niche of white stone
they have painted God's sister with wings
and a sword. I don't know who
she is slicing up, but it sure looks like
some ancient lover from the land of darkness.

Withered flowers cover her altar
and stubs of candles in tin cans
remember her darkest night.
Volcanic mountains loom above
in phallic fluted cliffs. A hummingbird
whirs in the branches. Invisible creatures
crackle the brush behind me
toward drifting zones of light.

For once I have really been a good boy.
I have fasted and prayed,
I have walked all the lonesome way
from the Pleistocene. I have carved
my flesh into poems.
But God's sister will not accept blackmail.
Sometimes she won't even accept devotion.
A sense of a shrug in the air.

John Oliver
Simon

It's up to her: the human daughter
of these powers,
who believes in nothing magical,
wanting to be free, wanting to fly,
manipulating the substances of earth
with practiced fingers. This music pulses
in her blood, the ticking of the years,
the cactus blooming on the mountain,
the eagles and jaguars ever watchful
in the den of the flesh of the living stone.

She turns me over slowly in her mind,
waiting for an answer.

has twice won the Greek National Prize for Poetry: second prize in 1958 for *Central Arcade* (he declined it), and first prize in 1983 for *Some Women*. His books written in English include *Hired Hieroglyphs* (Kayak 1970), *Diplomatic Relations* (Panjandrum 1971), and *Flash Boom* (Wire Press 1980). Poems have appeared in *Poetry* (Chicago), *Chicago Review*, Bantam's *Modern European Literature*, the *Penguin Anthology of Socialist Poetry*, and *Velocities*. In addition, Valaoritis edited the Greek review *Pali* from 1963 to 1967, and co-edited *Bastard Angel* with Harold Norse.

Valaoritis writes: ". . . all those whose opinion I cared for are dead. Eliot, Pound, Breton, Seferis, Michaux, Auden, Cyril Connoly, Andreas Embirikos,—with the exception of the Greek poet Nikos Engonopoulos and Harold Norse.... The present serialization of poetry is a curse. Everybody writes, nobody reads or listens. We have to re-learn to read and listen. Especially those who think they can write. For those who share with me my illusory universes—I have the warmest sympathy love and appreciation. Toward the rest: I am indifferent."

The editor was fortunate enough to hear "Poem Unlimited" read by the poet in 1985. It is a poem to hear, but *POLY* must be satisfied with presenting its first appearance in print.

Nanos
Valaoritis

The foreleg of a bowl of soup hits my jaw.

A very rusty joke hits the ceiling

A couple of shoe-strings make calls on their owner.

The colour on the wall beckons cordially.

A poster walks out on you.

Dyed hair becomes a living flame.

No "elephant" can open a can of "sardines" with his trunk.

New ideals fill up my stomach.

My toes clutch wildly as if they were about to drown.

Nothing looks down on me with a blue grin.

Alarm clocks with shattered teeth pronounce wrong.

Waking up dead is my favourite game.

The occasion calls for an oil-strike.

Electric eel caught up in a fragment of ossified lake.

The colour of your tits glows afar.

Candour wakes up the sleeping corridor with a gentle nudge.

A scene of desolation floats off in the dark.

Your locks lock me out of time.

Forged anonymity is no answer for the first time.

Everyone sings with wax in their ears.

Some are also tied by the throat to the past.

The battered building slowly sinks.

Catcalls wave their plumes from check-points inside your viewpoint. No
   laughter follows.

Automobiles turn over on their backsides and play dead.

The independence of twilight. The long prayer of freeways.

Most drivers are not aware of a hole in the sky,

In which all hope imaginable is engulfed.

Strangers come back from abroad,

Breathing new portholes into letter boxes.

Everyone treads on arithmetic.

Squirming coils of sound emerge from the inner ear.

The sanctuaries of toilets are being violated by the opposite sex.

Amazement holds me clasped by the waist.

Amplified light is rowing along the river bank.

Sunlight summons all bulbs to attention.

A green gas escapes from the mouths of orators,

Where a holocaust of words is in the making.

No bowl of rice can save a body of knowledge.
Angry looks carved by fire.
A bronze bust begins a lift-off.
Kindness has handles of ivory.
Scintillating secretaries of space.
Changes are ringing inside my head.
Watermills leave the joyful shores of a plain chant.
The conversation turns brown with side-burns.
Fireworks build a citadel of kisses.
Orifices leak unlocked quantities of space.
A ship's prow ploughs the frowning hillside.
A chorus of clouds blocks the ears of syllables.
I allowed myself to be caressed by strangers.
They are precocious to the point of courage.
All voices converge on a mid-atlantic masterpiece.
I hold a meeting in people's eyes.
A martyrdom of smiles faces canonization.
Frequent shudders are spattered on the forecast.
No one will be displayed for their good actions.
I feel I'm not boring enough to be understood.
Anyone can guess underdeveloped hair.
Don't mince your metaphores if you like meat-loaves.
Rinse and shave if you cannot do otherwise.
Outrage is not the only way out of eating. There are others.
If *you belong* don't stay there too long.
Pull their legs off if you can't stand on them.
Betray before becoming an accessory.
Lower yourself up to the highest standards.
Only smile when taken apart.
Secrets don't count. They only blush if blemished.
The long monotonous silence after noise.
I leap large quantities of myself to hide my concealment.
The dull substance of my spittle travels far without a croak.
Lend me the strong offense that windows in your breast.
Further South, guess what—no islands for sale.
A slice of genius is the onion skin of breathlessness.
A very rusty look hits the meaning.
Perspective travels faster than time.
There were fears for her afterlife.

Nanos
Valaoritis

Nanos
Valaoritis

Gentlemen, we have achieved what nothing else couldn't.
Hence, the great Goethe racked his brains.
The history of emotions is tedious enough without feelings.
Black birthdays cause an apoplectic moratorium.
The fear of words deals with the desire of things.
My eyes sting with the ill at ease that fills the room.
Marginal yes, although not mortal.
Thank you for manipulating ice-stardom to infrequency.
I passed through many Cyrano des of illusion.
The ultimate place is suddenly tyrannical.
Economize without wasting.
This line hovers slightly above the page.
Elevated by enthusiasm it is brought down by shot-gun.
There's nothing better to do, than anticipate.
The stamp of my actions are the warriors of my congregations.
the sun swarms of being able.
Without a guitar tuning remains occult.
I'm not really surprised to see you walking on the stage naked.
Even though you're not really flying as promised.
It's not a sword nor has it been sworn in yet.
All three walls converge to form a myth.
Nothing stands as stiff as some flowers.
To be nourished by thoughts the size of a mushroom.
Great piles of air swallowed by those whom thunders strikes.
What I believe in I have to laugh at if it threatens excellence.
The harpsichord strikes a repellent chord in the heart of prosewriting.
I'd appreciate some pretty face from someone.
Efforts are being made so that neither side will talk,
And not only to each other.
Not everyone is necessarily human.
Centripetal forces begin to pull us apart.
Centrifugal forces begin to bring us together.
We tend to levitate because we can't walk to the next stop.
It is easier on the whole to be a forerunner, in the aftermath.
Even if dreadful things won't happen you can count on it.
Is it possible to pass on information without eyelashes?
Come what may the road stubbornly lies on its back.
A house lies on its side too tired to stand up.
People are walking on all fours so as not to attract attention.

In a restaurant I order a meal for ten. What happened to the other nine?
As I enter the fog I discover there's no other madman hidden in it.
He offers me his tongue for half a spoon.
Thanks to him I will be able to cut my discoveries in two. *Nanos*
The feminine and the masculine sides are the least conspicuous. *Valaoritis*
A blow emerges from the lips of innocence.
A jargon full of animals strikes it rich.
I hear a clatter of overthrown cabbage.
I try to swallow but I'm mistaken. It won't go down.
My hand is glued to a glove I've never worn.
Under the circumstances it is safer to say that there's no latitude left.
As the fog becomes denser and denser it clears away.
The domains of thought are not the same as the domains of humans.
My luxury has been so distilled, that it displeases me.
He offers me part of himself to throw out of the window.
Was he in his right mind on the left side of his brain?

Has been editor or co-editor of *Portland Review Magazine*, *Star*Line*, *Lifeline*, and *Scene* (now *Alchemy*), and a regular columnist for *Hayakawa SF Magazine*, Tokyo. His poems and translations have been anthologized in *Burning With a Vision* (Owlswick 1984), *The Umbral Anthology of SF Poetry* (1982), and *Chrysalis 10* (Doubleday 1983). He has also frequently published in *Velocities* and *Eternity SF*. A long-time Oregonian, Van Troyer is at present living and writing in Japan. "The Myth of the Man at the Center" is a cycle of poems new for *POLY*.

THE MYTH OF THE MAN AT THE CENTER

A Cycle of Poems

Gene
Van Troyer

THE KNOWLEDGE OF LOSS

The man at the center
has the sky at night for his mind:
the stars still burn

but he has lately lost
his constellations
scans in vain
the tension of remoteness

hoping for a single line
to etch upon his eyes
a crosspoint of stability

as certain as
the cob-webbed corner
of his livingroom:
and the absolute shadow of space

sucks like loss of memory
at the ceiling of his brain
while grandfather clock

hands pointing years
not hours
drops ticks and tocks
that pendulate

around the silence
pound against the walls
like hammers

nailing in
the
stops

Inertia, grey duration
uncertain skies at morning
and clouds like omens
on intermittent winds

Gene
Van Troyer

doubt
is the off-spring of certainty
coupled with a Why.

There are purposes
like sand
and evidence of immutable
laws

in ambiguous words.
Doubt is a certain
hesitation, bedrock

riding out the quakes
and comets gashing
the heavens
disfiguring constellations

like the best of plans
foundations holding you up
while sinking in the sand.

Gene
Van Troyer

The man at the center
is questing for paintings on walls
in the liquid cavern
of his skull
where thoughts like glistery
shadowbats sound out the world
with electric calls.
There is no resting here
in these vast curled catacombs
if biotic mystery:
the residue of lives
and evolutionary eras past
still live in the blue dreamlight
that leaks from the turbulent nerves
and illuminates each cell:
there, thriving in their
helical abodes
the migrant codes
that swam up from their
precambrian mother lodes.
The twists and curves
of his uncertain
way
loop around
and turn the outside in.
His journey ends
where the membranes of his
eyes begin
staring inside out.
The only portraiture he sees—
the moon, the sun, the stars.
The hills. The trees
The cities and the seas.
The lines of his own face
looking back from a mirror.
The shapes of things in space
both near and far
reflected in the black pools
of his pupils.

They won't explain
themselves, as if
they're nothing.
He must write the rules
of order for himself.

*Gene
Van Troyer*

Gene
Van Troyer

1

Who is the man at
the center? He dreams every
night of his genes.

What are they like?
Swimming cells like tadpoles,
warmed in their migrant stream.

Does he even know
who he is? The woman moans
beside him in her sleep.

2

He knows who he is.
Where in the mirrors of his genes
does he live?

The woman moans in him
beside his sleep. Does he wonder what
unexed him into manhood?

He wonders who she is.
She is deeper than the cells.
How wide is the wall between them?

3

Does the woman in him moan
in their sleep? She dreams of the wall
of genes, universe wide, touch thin.

Gene
Van Troyer

What does she think?
He dreams of everything unfound. She
wants to hold his twin to her heart.

What does he dream?
She thinks of difference, and his cells
moan. They share the same ground.

4

Is there a man at the center?
He sees a face in the crystals of his genes.
Is the moaning woman at the center?

The man and woman are not sure
of centers. Does she wonder what unexed her
out of womanhood?

He dreams of genes, moaning in her sleep.
Where in the mirrors of his genes does she live?
She will awaken in his sleep.

Gene
Van Troyer

His skin feels
like the sail of a soaring kite
tautened in the thermals
of a time wind.

Higher and higher
on the negative heat, he rises
in the abyss of the
uncertain sky.

Clouds wait, pregnant
with yet to be formed shapes. Stars
wait for yet to be named
configurations.

Stars. Clouds. Wait.
Wait. The paralyzed imagination.
The blank sheet starved for
definition

wait. While
the forest of the valley below
recedes into the bowl
of life past.

The horror
assails him. Of bleak scarecrows
in naked fields. Bony branches
of fruitless yield.

The terror
hails him, he thinks it cries
for more, but he banks
away

rising higher
on the relentless wind
for everything that
waits for him

Gene
Van Troyer

everything felt:
the sun hot on his wing of skin. But
this time it will not
melt.

is interested in the overlap of science and the inner life, what science "discovers" and what the "individual" experiences. His poetry has been published in *Pacific Review*, *Plainsong*, and in anthologies *Burning With a Vision*, *Permutations: Readings in Science & Literature*, and *Eating the Menu: Anthology of Contemporary American Poetry* among others. He has been poetry editor of *Appalachian Journal*, and writer-in-residence at Marshall, Minnesota, and he now lives in San Diego, California. Zolynas's two books of poems are *Ten Poems of India* (Chapman College 1983) and *The New Physics* (Wesleyan University Press 1979).

Al
Zolynas

If coaxed, my mother will tell the story
of the Wheel of Fire from her girlhood
on her parents' farm in Lithuania.
But you must coax her
for the telling details, urge her to recall
the sequence of events, and
as in all the best stories, you
must take it on yourself, wear it, fill
it, sacrifice a portion of your
own life for its sake.

One mid-summer day, when my mother
was ten years old, she was left at the farm
while the rest of the family
went off to Sunday mass.
Somehow, she had hurt her foot
with a handsaw, and now it was swathed in bandages.

They left her in charge of a younger boy,
the son of one of the tenants,
a Petrukas or Vincukas—
diminutives for Peter and Vincent—she can't
remember which. Her stern but loving father
(the grandfather I never knew) told her
not to leave the house, not to go galavanting
around on her injured foot.

When the family—all the five sisters and brother
and parents—and the rest of the household
piled into the wagons and left for church,
my mother soon grew restless.
She decided she and Petrukas or Vincukas
would go pick flowers.

So, off they went to a nearby fallow field
full of waving daisies, she hobbling
on her bandaged foot, urging along the innocent
and now faceless Petrukas or Vincukas.
It was a hot day, and as they wandered further
and further from the house, the bouquets
of daisies growing in their hands,
they didn't notice the mushrooming storm clouds
until it was too late.

The wind suddenly picked up,
everything grew dark, and the lightning
began its primeval dance.
My mother looked towards the farmhouse
and saw a haystack catch fire,
apparently struck by lightning.

She began running to the farmhouse in fright,
her bandages unraveling, the younger
boy trailing behind her.

Then, as she tells it,
there was a tremendous clap of thunder
("Perkunas," as we say in Lithuanian,
which is both the word for thunder
and for the pagan god of thunder).
Petrukas or Vincukas cried out,
my mother stopped, turned, and witnessed
what she calls a Wheel of Fire
that rolled furiously along the ground
like a blazing bicycle wheel.
It seemed to run over or through
the boy, knocking him flat
on his back and singeing his hair and clothes.

He lay there, clothes smoking,
as my mother, terrified, ran back to him,
knelt and beat his smoldering shoulders
with her bare hands.

Al
Zolynas

Al
Zolynas

What happened next, she can't
remember exactly, but some farmhands
who had been bathing in the nearby river
ran up and attended the boy, now
conscious but dazed, and carried him
into the garden near the house.
There they dug a shallow trough,
lay him in it and buried
him up to his neck, his head
sticking out of the sod like some cabbage.
They did this to ''draw off'' the electricity
or the power of Perkunas
that had entered him—
all this, of course, in accordance
with the folk customs of that place and time.

The boy recovered, my mother was punished
for having disobeyed her father, and everyone
almost managed to talk
her out of her experience, suggesting
there was no Wheel of Fire, that it was lighting
after all, or something that had fallen
from the burning haystack.

But when my mother tells this story,
she gets what I call her ''gypsy face,'' that expression
half fearful, half knowing
with eyes that are focused on a place
a few light years right behind you,
a place you can't see
but have strong reason to suspect is there nonetheless.

So that's the story of my mother,
Petrukas or Vincukas, and the Wheel of Fire.
It happened a long time ago
on my grandfather's farm in Lithuania
right here on Planet Earth.

Born in 1939 in Chomutov, Czechoslovakia, Peter Loschan spent his childhood in German-occupied Sudetenland, and survived the bombardment of Dresden. Settling in Swabia, he attended Maristenschule Gymnasium, Mindelheim. In 1955, he emigrated to the United States and in 1957, began professional work as an industrial glassblower. He is now living and painting in the San Francisco area.

In 1957–8, Loschan studied at the California College of Arts and Crafts. He exhibited at *The Six Gallery*, San Francisco, with Manuel Neri, Kenneth Price, Mark diSuvero. Active in New York City in the early 1960s, he devoted himself to sculptures in laminated plywood, glass, metals, motorized constructions, and conceptual art. Since 1969, he has worked primarily in drawing and series-drawing, beam sculptures incorporating reflectors and bent-glass, and life-size figurative paintings.

Loschan is a regular participant in Berkeley's annual Actualist shows. He has had recent one-man-shows at Oakland's *10th Street Gallery*, and *Dolce* in Walnut Creek. His work for publication include drawings for *Proceedings of the Actualists* (Berkeley 1984), Andrew Joron and Robert Frazier's *A Measure of Calm* (Ocean View Books 1985), and cover and all interior drawings for *POLY*. For information about his current projects and works for sale, please contact Ocean View Books.

Taking the measure of the new speculative writing, especially poetry, will first of all require access to current and older works, both creative and critical, which have appeared. More and more, speculative poetry, at all levels of sophistication, is appearing in the mass circulation s-f digests. Though it will always stand somewhat apart, poetry is moving into the mainstream of science fiction, just as in a larger sense, poetry itself is re-entering the mainstream of contemporary literature. Meanwhile, small presses continue to publish the most challenging work without limiting themselves to safe, accepted, "accessible" forms. Since much important work has been published only in the small press, it is worthwhile to assemble in one place a list of essential books and articles. Some of number of these are now available directly from Ocean View Books. Others are listed with the necessary contact information.

VISUAL POETRY

The 1980s have seen a number of new developments in literature. The texture of these changes may be measured using *foundness* as a gauge. Visual poetry, like that in SCORE or KALDRON is *found* at the letter-form level. It is supported by a burgeoning regional influence in centers like San Francisco, Madison, and Los Angeles. A sample KALDRON is available for $5 from Karl Kempton, Box 7036, Halcyon CA 93420 – 7036. A sample SCORE is available for $5 from Craig Hill, 491 Mandana Blvd. 3, Oakland CA 94610.

SURREALISM

Against all odds, a contemporary surrealist scene maintains its tenuous toehold in the cliff of American publishing, with Philip Lamantia, Ivan Argüelles, Franklin Rosemont, and others. A sample of recent work must include Lamantia's *Meadowlark West*, $4.95 from your bookseller or from City Lights Books, 261 Columbus Avenue, San Francisco CA 94133, and Argüelles's *The Tattooed Heart of the Drunken Sailor*, available for $4 from ABRAXAS, 2518 Gregory Street, Madison WI 53711.

Xexoxial Editions publishes *non-idiomatic* books of interest. Send a
SASE to: miekal and, 1341 Williamson, Madison WI, 53703. Toronto
is home to a number of innovating writers, including *POLY* contributors
Mark Laba and Yves Troendle. A good contact and starting point is the
prolific SPIDER PLOTS IN RAT HOLES, which produces fine books and
ephemera at great prices. Send $2.50 U.S. for a sample to: J.W. Curry,
1357 Lansdowne Ave., Toronto, Ontario M6H 3Z9 Canada.

SCIENCE FICTION

There are related experiments taking place in science fiction and fan-
tasy. William Burroughs and Brion Gysin's *The Third Mind* (Viking 1978)
is an introduction to the cut-up method they pioneered. The typographic
novels of Max Frisch and Jessica Amanda Salmonson's clip-texts are
other examples. See for example, Frisch's *Man in the Holocene* (Har-
court Brace 1980) and Salmonson's superb little book *Slide Show*, which
is available for $2 from Duck's-Foot Tree Press, Box 20610, Seattle WA
98102.

FOUND TEXTS

Most modern newspapers, though useless for their intended purposes,
are compendia of the *found*, with bizarre wire service "news" items
(passed on unchecked), society spleen, homophobia, techno-crackery
and bus plunge filler. For many of us this is the *real* science fiction.

THE MAGAZINE OF SPECULATIVE POETRY

The outspoken voice of editors Roger Dutcher and Mark Rich. Imperative
reading for its range of expression and unique editorial flavor. A sam-
ple copy is available for $2.00 from Mark Rich, Box 564, Beloit WI 53511.

Since 1981, a unique essential voice of the new poetry. The first five issues of this seminal journal, in a handsome cloth slipcase with a new introduction by editor Andrew Joron, Tom Disch, Joe Haldeman, Adam Cornford, Kim Stanley Robinson, Suzette Haden Elgin, and many others. $16.95 from Ocean View Books.

T H E   B R U C E   B O S T O N   O M N I B U S

Five volumes handsomely slipcased: *Jackbird, She Comes When You're Leaving, All the Clocks Are Melting, Alchemical Texts* and *Nuclear Futures*. The complete small press fiction and poetry of Bruce Boston. Five volumes, 210 pages, illustrated, $16.95 from Ocean View Books.

T H E   O C E A N   V I E W   D O U B L E S   S E R I E S

Each volume in this series joins a single work of speculative writing with a second text by a writer working outside the genre. The first book in the series, *Prayer Wheels of Bluewater/Co-Orbital Moons*, presents the typeface Lucida, created by Charles Bigelow and Kris Holmes, in its first book appearance. Bigelow, a professor of art and computer science at Stanford University, is a leading exponent of digital typography. He has also been an award-winning printer of letterpress books, and a small press publisher. Bigelow and Holmes designed the intricate capitals for Andrew Hoyem's Arion Press *Moby Dick*. For information on upcoming titles, contact Ocean View Books, Box 4148, Mountain View CA 94040.

LITERARY

A fellow scribbler shows me his latest poem,
Hands me the sheet
And the letters, too small to read with the naked eye,
Are moving indeed: mites
That crawl here and there, shifty,
One or two right over the edge of the paper.
Does it matter, I ask, if they disappear?
No, he says, there are others to take their places.

Through strong lenses I can follow
Their permutations, lively enough, suggestive,
Recoiling only when the more sinister kinds
Leave the page and threaten my skin.

Michael Hamburger

POLY was designed by Steve Renick of Anselm Design, and set in Bookman and Helvetica, with cover and interior artwork by Peter Loschan. Composition was by Richard Miller and the staff of Weekly Graphics, Palo Alto, California, and the book was manufactured by Malloy Lithographing, Inc., of Ann Arbor, Michigan. Jennifer Ballentine, of Ocean View Books, was managing editor. Two hundred copies of *POLY* have been cloth bound in a special edition.

Ocean View Books

Box 4148

Mountain View, California